March of America Facsimile Series

Number 19

Henry Hudson's Voyages

Samuel Purchas

Henry Hudson's Voyages

from Purchas His Pilgrimes
by Samuel Purchas

ANN ARBOR

UNIVERSITY MICROFILMS, INC.

A Subsidiary of Xerox Corporation

Purchas His Pilgrimes, a collection of travel accounts, was assembled by an English clergyman, Samuel Purchas, and printed in 1625. The section from the third part reproduced here describes the four voyages of the English navigator, Henry Hudson, who, under English and Dutch auspices, sought for a northern passage to the Orient between 1607 and 1611. Although the river, the strait, and the bay which bear Hudson's name indicate some of the regions in which he sailed, he was not their discoverer. Nevertheless, Hudson's explorations in these northerly latitudes added greatly to the store of geographical knowledge. As an immediate consequence of his voyages, the English established fur trapping posts along the Hudson Bay, and the Dutch laid claim to the Hudson River Valley.

Hudson's first two voyages of 1607 and 1608 were sponsored by the English Muscovy Company. As Hudson vainly sought for a passage across the North Pole, his journals are replete with entries showing the difficult conditions under which the voyages were made. "Our shroude and sayles frozen," "thick fogge," "raw cold" were expressions often repeated. Yet there were lighter moments too. When the crew reported seeing a mermaid, Hudson duly recorded the incident, noting that "her body [was] as big as one of us; her skin very white; and long haire hanging downe behind."

The Dutch East India Company sponsored Hudson's third voyage in 1609. It was on this trip that he sailed into the Hudson River and explored as far as the site of what is today Albany. As he sailed back out of the river he commented that one side was called "Manna-hata. There we saw no people to trouble us." On the passage home Hudson stopped at Dartmouth, where the English authorities refused to allow him to proceed to Holland. They informed Hudson that he and the other Englishmen in his crew ought to henceforth serve their own country, not the Dutch.

A new company was formed in England soon after to finance Hudson's fourth search for a northern passage. Departing from London in 1610, Hudson eventually passed through the Hudson Strait and arrived in Hudson Bay. With his ship locked in ice, he and his men spent the winter in James Bay. The extreme hardships endured by the crew caused some of them to mutiny in the spring of 1611. Hudson, his son, and a few others who remained loyal were set adrift in a small boat while the ship sailed back to England. An expedition sent out from England the following year to search for Hudson and his party could find no trace of them.

These accounts of Hudson's voyages were written in some cases by Hudson himself and in some cases by members of the crew. The editor, Samuel Purchas, remarked in a prefatory epistle to the Bishop of Lincoln that his own interest in exploration dated back to his school days at Cambridge. Purchas said of himself that "without travelling hee hath travelled ever since." Purchas collected journals and records of voyages to far-off lands in a manner similar to that of Richard Hakluyt. Although Purchas was often a careless editor, his collection is an extremely important source. Often his published accounts of voyages are all that have survived, the original manuscripts having been lost. An interesting study of Hudson is that of Llewelyn Powys, *Henry Hudson* (New York, 1928). *The Dictionary of National Biography* contains additional information about the editor, Samuel Purchas.

Henry Hudson's Voyages

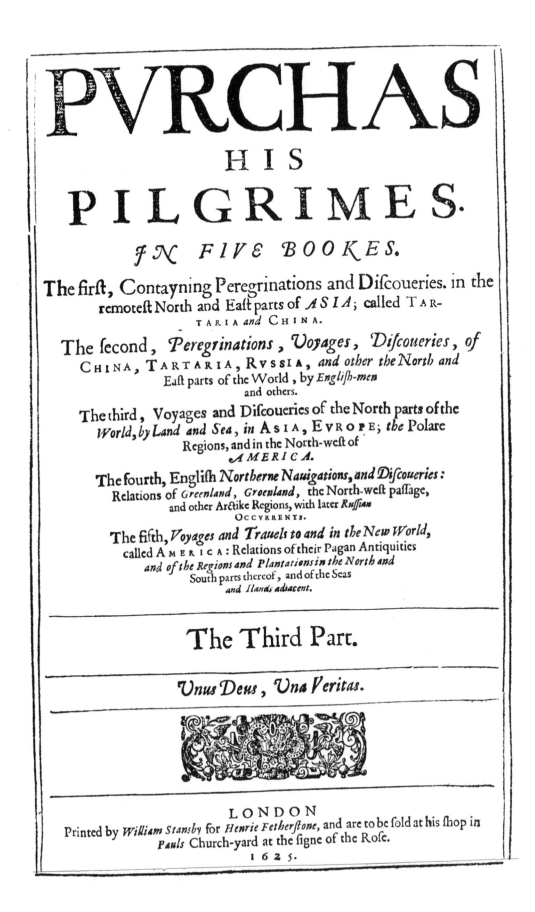

PVRCHAS

HIS
PILGRIMES.

IN FIVE BOOKES.

The firſt, Contayning Peregrinations and Diſcoueries. in the remoteſt North and Eaſt parts of *ASIA*; called TAR-TARIA *and* CHINA.

The ſecond, *Peregrinations, Voyages, Diſcoueries, of* CHINA, TARTARIA, RVSSIA, *and other the North and* Eaſt parts of the World, by *Engliſh-men* and others.

The third, Voyages and Diſcoueries of the North parts of the World, by Land and Sea, in ASIA, EVROPE; *the* Polare Regions, and in the North-weſt of *AMERICA.*

The fourth, Engliſh *Northerne Nauigations, and Diſcoueries :* Relations of *Greenland, Groenland,* the North-weſt paſſage, and other Arctike Regions, with later *Ruſſian* OCCVRRENTS.

The fifth, *Voyages and Trauels to and in the New World,* called AMERICA : Relations of their Pagan Antiquities *and of the Regions and Plantations in the North and* South parts thereof, and of the Seas *and Ilands adiacent.*

The Third Part.

Vnus Deus, Vna Veritas.

LONDON
Printed by *William Stansby* for *Henrie Fetherſtone,* and are to be ſold at his ſhop in *Pauls* Church-yard at the ſigne of the Roſe.
1625.

TO
THE RIGHT
HONORABLE, AND
RIGHT REVEREND
FATHER IN
GOD:
IOHN,

Lord Biſhop of LINCOLNE, Lord *Keeper*
of the GREAT SEALE of
ENGLAND, &c.

Right Reuerend and Honourable :

Heſe PILGRIMS deliuering a Hiſtorie of the World in their owne Trauels by Sea and Land, not onely needed authoritie from the Admiraltie, but fearing ſuſpition of *Riot* without warrantable aſſemblie, become humble Sutors for your Lordſhips fauour. So ſhall they in the approbation of both (to apply by a warrant of *Ego dixi, dij eſtis*, the Patriarchs Gen.28.12. myſticall Dreame to our Hiſtoricall purpoſe) finde a *Scala Cœli* to aſcend from the ground where they are proſtrate Petitioners, to the Princes Highneſſe, whence authoriſed they may againe *deſcend* and become the Commons of Common Readers. Order requires a *Medium* betwixt Princely Height and his Lowlineſſe, whoſe function is alſo tearmed *Holy Orders*, as further tying him to that equall inequalitie; wherein hee beſeecheth your Lordſhip

as by speciall Office and in proprietie to owne that which hee hath presumed to offer to the Prince in *Capite*, *Quemadmodum sub optimo rege omnia Rex imperio possidet, Domini dominio. Ad reges potestas pertinet, ad singulos proprietas.*

Many are the reasons which moued the Author to obtrude his PILGRIMS on your Lordship; because he is deeply obliged yours for former fauours, euen then when you were initiated in the Mysteries of Honour (learning by seruice to Command) in the Discipline of that Honorable worthy Lord Chancellor EGERTON! because some conceptions of this Worke were in your Honourable Iurisdiction of *Westminster*, whither left some traduce *Trauellers* for *Vagrants*, they returne in hope of *Sanctuarie*, or not so much trusting to ancient Liberties, as your Lordships liberall respect to literate endeauours : because these Trauellers aduenturing the world, seeke like *Iacob* at his going and returne, a Reuerend Fathers *Blessing* and *Confirmation*. The Author likewise being called on for his promised *Europe*, submits himselfe to your Lordships Order, heere tendring of that debt, what hee is able in readie payment. The worke it selfe also being a Librarie in this kind, presents it selfe to your Honour, the Founder of two famous Libraries ; one in *Westminster*, (where the Stones renued Fabrikes speake your magnificence) the other in that famous Nurserie of Arts and Vertue Saint IOHNS Colledge in *Cambridge*, which sometime knew you a hopefull Sonne, but now acknowledgeth your Lordship a happie Father, where also the Author first conceiued with this Trauelling *Genius*, whereof without trauelling hee hath trauelled euer since. Learning, the Aduancer of your Honour, hath secured her welwillers not to bee reiected in whatsouer indeauours (*Scribimus indocti, doctiq,*) to aduance Learning. The greatnesse of Nature to goodnesse of Nature, varietie of Estates to a prime Pillar of State, the Historie of Religions to a Religious Prelate, of Antiquities to an Antiquarie, cannot bee altogether vnwelcome ; that I mention not the dependance of *London* Ministers Liuings (*fined* by the Times iniquitie) on your Lordships equall Sentence. These Causes haue moued, One hath inforced ; these PILGRIMES are your Seruants, fitly so called *à Seruando*, saued by your Lordships hand when they were giuing vp the ghost, despairing through a fatall stroke of euer seeing light.

Most humbly therefore, sue vnto your Honour, these PILGRIMES for acknowledgement, esteeming your Lordships Name in fore-front a cognisance of blest Libertie and best Seruice ; now when *Ianus* sends many with gratefull emulations to present their acclamations of a *New Yeere*, presenting (a wordie rather then worthy Present) a world, yea, a New world, in great part one Age younger to mens knowledge then *America*, sometimes stiled by that Name. I had written other Causes of my addresse to your Honour, but dare not proceed to interrupt others more weightie ; In all humble earnestnesse beseecheth, now in this Festiuall time, the Author with his PILGRIMES to finde Hospitall

[margin notes:]
Senec.Benef.l.7. cap.4.

Gen.18.& 22. 20.

Aug.de CD. lib. 19.cap.5.

tall entertainment, not at your Honours table, where Great affaires of Church and State are feasted (except some recreation sometimes permit) but with Schollers and Gentlemen in the Hall, which will welcome such Guests as your Lordship shall Countenance. So shall you encourage euer to pray for the increase of
your Lordships happinesse
in the
Happie Seruice of his
MAIESTIE,

Your Lordships

most bounden,

SAMVEL PVRCHAS.

Auguſt.

The ſixt of Auguſt, I tooke the Skiffe and ſeuen men to fetch the Shallop to the Coue, that Maſter *Welden* had left in a Coue, on the North-weſt ſide of the Iland, the laſt of Iuly. When I came to the place, conſidering I was neere the North ſide, where we commonly make our Voyage, and alſo deſired by Maſter *Welden*, if I could goe, to doe ſo, I went thither, and found about fiue and fortie as good headed beaſts for Teeth, as euer I ſaw. Wee had no more Launces to kill them with all, but two, I tooke one, and a luſtie fellow that was our Cooper had the other: we had not killed paſt ten but his Lance brake. Then I ſlue all the reſt in leſſe then two houres; and wee tooke their Teeth; and the next day by a Weſt Sunne wee came aboord the *Paul* with them.

Note.

The eight day, wee got the Southermoſt Point of the Iland: where wee rid all that day. Their Skiffe from their long Boats ſterne, and we manned our Boat to fetch her againe: but then roſe ſuch a fogge, that we had like to haue loſt both our Boats and men; but they got to the ſhip againe with mucl adoe.

The ninth day, it was calme; but wee had ſuch a fogge, that wee could not ſee two Cables length from the ſhip. And about eight of the Clocke at night, wee loſt our Skiffe altogether.

The tenth day, we had a little Wind at North-weſt and by Weſt. Then ſeeing no amendment of the weather, wee left the ſhip of *Hull* behind vs in the Iland, and about ſixe of the Clocke ſet ſayle for *England*, and arriued ſafely at *London* the laſt of Auguſt, 1609. Bleſſed bee God.

10

20

A *Voyage performed to the Northwards,* Anno 1603. *in a ſhip of the burthen of fiftie tunnes, called the* Grace, *and ſet forth at the coſt and charges of the Worſhipfull* FRANCIS CHERIE. *Written by* WILLIAM GORDEN; *being the firſt Voyage to* Cherie *Iland; which came to my hands ſince the former (or rather later Voyages) were in the Preſſe.*

30

An Iland.

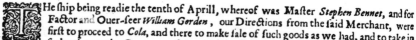

He ſhip being readie the tenth of Aprill, whereof was Maſter *Stephen Bennet*, and for Factor and Ouer-ſeer *William Gorden*, our Directions from the ſaid Merchant, were firſt to proceed to *Cola*, and there to make ſale of ſuch goods as we had, and to take in ſuch other as the Countrey of *Lappia* did affoord, and then to proceed vpon ſome Diſcouerie. Wherefore omitting our Iourney to *Cola*, as a matter of ſmall importance, being ſo well knowne before, after our Affaires ended, we were readie to proceed forward. But our men not being hired thereunto would haue refuſed, if there had not beene made an agreement by meanes of *Ioſias Logan*, who was to lye there as Factor for Maſter *Cherie*, the Maſter and my ſelfe, partly with promiſes, partly with gifts. And thus ſetting forward the ſixt of Auguſt, from the Riuer of *Cola*, being determined to haue ſayled into 80. degrees of latitude, if nothing did hinder vs; or if we did not light vpon ſome land: our determination was hindered by meanes of meeting with an Iland, and likewiſe the yeere being farre ſpent, keeping our courſe from the Weſt end of *Kilden*, to the Ilands of *Ward-houſe*, which wee paſſed the tenth of Auguſt with little wind; then directing our courſe North North-weſt, the wind at South-weſt eaſie wind, ſo that the eleuenth day we did reckon our ſelues to haue ſayled twentie leagues North-weſt. The twelfth day, it was moſt part calme and foggie. The thirteenth day, it was cleere, and the wind at South, and we had ſayled twentie two leagues North North-weſt. The fourteenth day, the wind at Eaſt, we kept our courſe and ſayled ten leagues, and the ſame day being thicke and foggie, we had thought wee had ſeene Land about foure of the clocke in the after-noone, bearing from vs Weſt North-weſt, and North-weſt by W'eſt, but ſayling towards it three houres, keeping ſtill his forme, and not altering till the wind increaſing, cauſed it to fade away (for it was no other then a banke of fogges) after we had ſayled three leagues changing our courſe, we ſayled then fifteene dayes twentie leagues, North-weſt and by North, ſtill hauing cloſe weather, that we could not make any obſeruation. The ſixteenth day in the morning, at two of the clock, we did ſee two great high Hils, which did ſeeme to vs aboue the Clouds, and did ſeeme very neere, but we found it otherwiſe for ſayling towards it, we found it further then we did expect, for it was ſixe of the clocke at night before wee could come neere vnto the Land, where wee anchored in thirtie fathomes. In which time we could not ſayle leſſe then eighteene leagues North and by Weſt. That night our Maſter knowing, better what did belong vnto thoſe Affaires, would not ſuffer the Boat to goe aland till the morning: which was the ſeuenteenth day of Auguſt, and before our going aland, the Maſter cauſed a ſhanke of Lines to bee ſhot for, to toy for fiſh, and then he and my ſelfe with foure of our Company went aland. Firſt, vpon a little Iland neere adjoyning, where we had much adoe to get to our Boat againe, by reaſon of the ſteepnes

40

50

60

of the Rockes : then we went on shoare vpon the Mayne, where at our comming on Land, wee did see two Foxes, one White, the other Blacke. Thus spending most part of the day, wee returned aboord our ship without any profit : only one of our men tooke vp a piece of Lead, and I found a piece of a Morses Tooth, by which we perceiued that the Sea Morses did vse thither, but the time for that yeere was past, for we did see none. After our comming aboord, hauing haled the Line, we found nothing but one but fish thereon, wherefore presently weighing Anchor, we sayled West to see if we could haue any true obseruation, the next day which wee had, and found our selues to bee in 74. degrees 30. minutes. The same day directing our course for *London,* where we arriued the tenth of September, by Gods helpe, in health and safetie.

10

Chap. XIIII.

Diuers Voyages and Northerne Discoueries of that worthy irrecouerable Discouerer Master Henry Hvdson. *His Discouerie toward the North Pole, set forth at the charge of certaine Worshipfull Merchants of* London, *in May* 1607. *Written partly by* Iohn Playse *one of the Company, and partly by* H. Hvdson.

20

Nno 1607. Aprill the nineteenth, at Saint *Ethelburge* in Bishops Gate street, did communicate with the rest of the Parishioners these persons Seamen, purposing to goe to sea foure dayes after, for to discouer a Passage by the North Pole to *Iapan* and *China.* First, *Henry Hudson* Master. Secondly, *William Colines* his Mate. Thirdly, *Iames Young.* Fourthly, *Iohn Colman.* Fittly, *Iohn Cooke.* Sixtly, *Iames Beubery.* Seuenthly, *Iames Skrutton.* Eightly, *Iohn Pleyce.* Ninthly, *Thomas Baxter.* Tenthly, *Richard Day.* Eleuenthly, *Iames Knight.* Twelfthly, *Iohn Hudson* a Boy.

The first of May 1607. we weyed Anchor at *Grauesend,* and on Tuesday the sixe and twentieth day in the morning, we made the Iles of *Shotland,* and at noone we were in 60. degrees 12. minutes, and sixe leagues to the Eastward of them : the Compasse had no variation. We had sixtie foure fathomes at our sounding, blacke, ozie, sandie, with some yellow shels. Our ship made more way then we did suppose. On Saturday the thirtieth of May, by our obseruation we were in 61. degrees 11. minutes, This day I found the Needle to incline 79. degrees vnder the Horizon. For foure dayes space we made very little way by contrary winds.

On Thursday the fourth of Iune, we were by our obseruation still in 61. degrees and 14. minutes, eight and twentie or thirtie leagues from the Norther part of *Shotland*: the Land bearing by our Accompt East and by North off vs, I found variation in fiue degrees Westerly.

The seuenth of Iune, wee were in 63. degrees 25. minutes. The eighth, all the fore-noone we had a fresh gale Southerly; we steered away North and by West, and by obseruation we were in 65. degrees 27. minutes.

The eleuenth, wee saw sixe or seuen Whales neere our shippe : wee were in sixtie seuen degrees thirtie minutes. About fiue of the clocke, the winde came vp at North-east and by East; wee steered away North North-west with a fresh gale all the night at East. The twelfth, the winde was at East North-east, a stiffe gale, wee steered away as afore, and accounted wee had runne by this day noone thirtie leagues. In the after-noone wee steered away North and by West fifteene leagues, all the night prooued a great fogge with much wind.

The thirteenth, betweene one and two in the morning, we saw some Land on head of vs, and some Ice : and it being a thicke fogge, we steered away Northerly, and hauing much wind wee stood away South and by East, sixe or eight leagues. Our sayle and shroudes did freeze, At eight in the morning it cleered vp, the wind being at North-east and by East, with much wind wee were hardly able to maintayne a sayle. This was a very high Land, most part couered with Snow. The neather part was vncouered. At the top it looked reddish, and vnderneath a blackish Clay, with much Ice lying about it. The part which we saw when wee cast about, trended East and West : And the Norther part which we saw, trended North-east and by North, and North-east : and the length which wee saw was nine leagues : wee saw much Fowle. Also wee saw a Whale close by the shoare. We called the Head-land which we saw, *Younga Cape*; and neere it standeth a very high Mount like a round Castle, which wee called, the *Mount of Gods Mercie.* All the after-noone, and all the Euening it rained. At eight in the Euening we cast about, and steered all night North and by West, and sometimes North North-west.

The fourteenth, being neere the Land we had Snow. At foure in the morning, the wind vering Northerly, we cast about and stood South-east and by South. This day wee had much wind and raine, we shorted sayle being neere the Land. The fifteenth, in the morning it blowed so much wind at North-east, that wee were not able to maintayne any sayle, wee then strooke a hull,

Margin notes:
May.
The Iles of Shotland.
No variation.
61.degrees 11 minutes.
The inclination of the Needle.
Iune.

65.degrees 27. minutes.
67. degrees 30 minutes.

Youngs Cape.
The Mount of Gods mercie.
Snow, &c.

hull, and let our ship driue, wayting for a fitter wind; this night was very much raine. The sixteenth, was much wind at North-east. The seuenteenth, we set sayle at noone, we steered away
East and by South, and East South-east. The eighteenth, in the afternoone a fine gale South-
east, which toward the Eeuening increased, and we steered North-east three Watches, twelue
leagues. The nineteenth we steered away North North-east sixteene leagues. At noone wee
had raine with fogge. From twelue to foure we steered North North-east eight leagues, and did
account our selues in seuentie degrees neerest hand: purposing to see whether the Land which
we made the thirteenth day, were an Iland or part of *Groneland*. But then the fogge increased
very thicke with much wind at South, which made vs alter our course, and to shorten our sayle,
and we steered away North-east. Being then as we supposed, in the Meridian of the same land, 10
hauing no obseruation since the eleuenth day, and lying a hull from the fifteenth to the seuenteenth day, wee perceiued a current setting to the South-west. This day wee saw three Whales
neere our ship, and hauing steered away North-east almost one watch, fiue leagues, the Sea was
growne euery way: we supposed wee were thwart of the North-east part of that Land which
we made the thirteenth day, and the current setting to wind-ward. The reason that mooued vs
to thinke so, was, that after we had sayled fiue or sixe leagues in this Sea, the wind neither increasing nor dulling, we had a pleasant and smooth Sea. All this night was foggie with a good
gale of wind, we steered away North-east vntill the next day at noone, and sayled in that course
twentie leagues.

The twentieth, all the morning was a thicke fogge with the winde at South: wee steered 20
North-east till noone. Then we changed our course, and steered away North North-east, hoping
for an open Sea in our course to fall with the bodie of *Newland*. This day at two in the after-

Note.
Land on their
Larboord.

noone it cleered vp, and wee saw the Sunne, which wee had not seene since the second of this
moneth. Hauing steered North North-east, two watches and an halfe, fifteene or sixteene
leagues wee saw Land on our Larboord, about foure leagues off vs, trending as wee could ghesse

Many Fowles.
Much drift Ice.
* To loose, is to
keepe close to
the wind: too-
mer cont.

North-east and South-west. We steered away East North-east, the wind at South a good gale,
but reasonable cleere: wee saw many Birds with blacke backes, and white bellies in forme much
like a Ducke: we saw also many pieces of Ice driuing at the Sea. We * loofed for one and went
roomer for another. And this morning about foure, a thicke fogge we saw a head of vs.

The one and twentieth, in the morning we steered North-east, and East North-east two wat- 30
ches, fiue or sixe leagues. Then it grew thicke fogge. And we cast about, and steered North-east

* To tacke the
ship, is to bring
her head about
to lye the o-
ther way.

and East North-east two watches, sixe leagues, finding wee were embayed. The wind came at
East South-east a little gale: we * tacked about and lay South. All this night was a thicke fog
with little wind, East we lay with the stemme.

Land not co-
uered with
Snow.

The two and twentieth, in the morning it cleered vp, being calme about two or three of the
clocke: after we had a prettie gale, and we steered away East and by North three leagues. Our
obseruation was in 72. degrees 38. minutes, and changing our course, we steered North-east, the
wind at South-east a prettie gale. This morning when it cleered vp, we saw the Land, trending
neere hand East North-east, and West South-west, esteeming our selues from it twelue leagues. It
was a mayne high Land, nothing at all couered with snow: and the North part of that 40
mayne high Land was very high Mountaynes, but we could see no snow on them. We accounted
by our obseruation the part of the mayne Land, lay neerest hand in 73. degrees. The many fogs
and calmes with contrary winds, and much Ice neere the shoare, held vs from farther Discouery
of it. It may bee objected against vs as a fault, for haling so Westerly a course. The chiefe cause
that mooued vs thereunto, was our desire to see that part of *Groneland*, which (for ought that we
know) was to any *Christian* vnknowne: and wee thought it might as well haue beene open Sea
as Land, and by that meanes our passage should haue beene the larger to the Pole: and the hope
of hauing a Westerly wind, which would be to vs a landerly wind if wee found Land. And
considering wee found Land contrarie to that which our Cards make mention of; we accounted
our labour so much the more worth. And for ought that wee could see, it is like to bee a good 50
Land, and worth the seeing.

On the one and twentieth day, in the morning while we steered our course North North-east,
we thought we had embayed our selues, finding Land on our Larboord, and Ice vpon it, and many great pieces of Drift Ice: we steered away North-east, with diligent looking out euery cleere
for Land, hauing a desire to know whether it would leaue vs to the East, both to know the
bredth of the Sea, and also to shape a more Northerly course. And considering wee knew no
name giuen to this Land, wee thought good to name it, *Hold with hope*, lying in 73. degrees of
latitude.

The Sunne was on the Meridian on the South part of the Compasse, neerest hand. Heere is

The Land of
Hold with Hope
in 73. degrees.

to bee noted that when we made *The Mount of Gods Mercie*, and *Youngs Cape*, the Land was 60
couered with snow for the most part, and extreame cold, when wee approached neere it: But
this Land was very temperate to our feeling. And this likewise is to be noted, that being two
dayes without obseruation; notwithstanding, our lying a hull by reason of much contrary wind,
yet our obseruation and dead reckoning were within eight leagues together, our shippe beeing

before vs eight leagues. This night vntill next morning prooued little Winde.

The three and twentieth, in the morning we had an hard gale on head of vs, with much rayne that fell in very great drops, much like our Thunder showers in *England*; wee tacked about and stood East Northerly with a short sayle, to our feeling it was not so cold as before we had it. It was calme from noone to three of the clocke with fogge. After the winde came vp at East and East South-east, we steered away North-east with the fogge and rayne. About seuen or eight of the clocke, the winde increased with extreame fogge, wee steered away with short sayle East North-east, and sometimes East and by North. About twelue at mid-night, the wind came vp at South-west, we steered away North, being reasonable cleere weather.

The foure and twentieth, in the morning about two of the clocke, the Masters mate thought he saw Land on the Larboord, trending North North-west Westerly, and the longer we ranne North, the more it fell away to the West, and did thinke it to bee a mayne high Land. This day the wind being Westerly, we steered away North, and by obseruation wee were in 73. degrees nearest hand. At noone we changed our course, and steered away North and by East, and at our last obseruation, and also at this, we found the Meridian all Leeward on the South and by West, Westerly part of the Compasse, when we had sayled two Watches eight leagues. *A mayne high Land.*

The fiue and twentieth, the wind scanted and came vp at North North-west, we lay North-east two Watches 8. leagues. After the wind became variable betweene the North-east and the North, we steered away East and by North, and sometimes East, we had thicke fogge. About noone three Granpasses played about our shippe. This After-noone the wind vered to the East and South-east, we haled away North and by East. This night was close weather, but small fogge (we vse the word *Night* for distinction of time, but long before this the Sunne was alway aboue the Horizon, but as yet we could neuer see him vpon the Meridian North.) This Night being by our accompt in the Latitude of 75. degrees, we saw small flockes of Birds, with blacke Backes and white Bellies, and long speare Tayles. We supposed that Land was not farre off, but we could not discrie any, with all the diligence which we could vse, being so close weather, that many times we could not see sixe or seuen leagues off. *75. Degrees: Land not farre off.*

The sixe and twentieth, in the morning was close weather, we had our wind and held our course as afore. This day, our obseruation was 76. degrees 38. minutes, and we had Birds of the same sort as afore, and diuers other of that colour, hauing red Heads; that we saw when we first made the Mount of *Gods Mercy* in *Greenland*, but not so many. After we steered away North and by East: two VVatches 10. leagues, with purpose to fall with the Souther part of *Newland*, ac-counting our selues 10. or 12. leagues from the Land. Then wee stood away North-east one VVatch fiue leagues. *76. degrees 38. minutes.*

The seuen and twentieth, about one or two of the clocke in the morning we made *Newland*, being cleere weather on the Sea; but the Land was couered with fogge, the Ice lying very thick all along the shoare for 15. or 16. leagues which we saw. Hauing faire wind wee coasted it in a very pleasing smooth sea, and had no ground at an hundred fathoms, foure leagues from the shoare. This day at noone, wee accounted we were in 78. degrees, and we stood along the shoare. This day was so foggie, that we were hardly able to see the Land many times, but by our account we were neare *Vogel Hooke*. About eight of the clocke this Eeuening, we purposed to shape our course from thence North-west. Heere is to bee noted, that although we ranne along neere the shoare, we found no great cold, which made vs thinke, that if we had beene on shoare the place is temperate. Holding this North-west course, about ten of the clocke at night, we saw great store of Ice on head off vs, bearing Wester off vs; which we could not goe cleere off with the foresayd course. Then we tact about, and stood away betweene the South and the South-east, as much desirous to leaue this Land as we were to see it. *Greenland or Newland disco-uered.* *78. Degrees.* *Vogel Hooke.* *Temperate ayre.*

The eight and twentieth, was a hard gale of wind all the fore-noone betweene the South and the South-west. We shaped our course   , we did it to bee farther from the Ice and Land. It pleased God that about twelue of the clocke this night it cleered vp, and we found that we were betweene the Land and the Ice; *Vogel Hooke* then bearing nearest hand East off vs. Then we tacked about, and stood in for the shoare, hauing Sea-roome between the Ice and the Land. The nine and twentieth, at foure in the morning the wind at North-east, a pretie gale, we thought best to shorten our way, so we tacked about and stood North North-west, the wind a little increasing. About twelue at noone, we saw Ice a head off vs; we cast about again, and stood away East South-east with very much wind, so that we shortned our sayles for the space of two Watches. Then about eight this Eeuening, we strucke a Hull, and it proued the hardest storme that we had in this Voyage. The thirtieth, in the morning was stormie; about noone it ceased, at seuen in the Eeuening it proued almost calme.

The first of Iuly, all the fore-noone the wind was at South-east, we stood North-east for the shoare, hoping to finde an open Sea betweene the shoare and the Ice. About noone wee were embayed with Ice, lying betweene the Land and vs. By our obseruation we were in 78. degrees 42. minutes, whereby we accounted we were thwart of *The great Indraught*. And to free our selues of the Ice, we steered betweene the South-east and South, and to the Westward, as *Iuly.* *78. degrees 42. minutes.*

we could haue fea ; And about fix, this Euening it pleafed God to giue vs cleere weather; and we found we were fhot farre into the Inlet, being almoft a Bay, and enuironed with very highMountaynes, with low Land lying betweene them ; wee had no ground in this Bay at an hundred fathoms. Then being fure where we were, we fteered away Weft, the wind at South-eaft and calme, and found all our Ice on the Norther fhoare, and a cleare Sea to the Southward.

The great Inlet.

The fecond, it pleafed God to giue vs the wind at North-eaft, a faire gale, with cleere weather, the Ice being to the Northward off vs, and the weather fhoare, and an open Sea to the Southwards vnder our Lee. We held on our courfe North-weft till twelue of the clocke ; hauing fayled in that courfe 10. leagues, and finding the Ice to fall from vs to the   , we gaue thankes to God, who maruelloufly preferued vs from fo many dangers, amongft fo huge a quantitie of Ice and Fogge. We fteered away North-weft, hoping to be free from Ice, we had obferuation 78. degrees 56. minutes, we fell with Ice againe, and trended it as it lay betweene the Weft and South South-eaft. The third, we had obferuation 78. degrees 33. minutes. This day wee had our fhrouds frozen, it was fearching cold, we alfo trended the Ice, not knowing whether we were cleare or not, the wind being at North.

78. Degrees 56. Minutes.
78. degrees 33. minutes.

The fourth, was very cold, and our fhroudes and fayles frozen, we found we were farre in the Inlet. The wind being at North, we beare vp and ftood South South-eaft, and South and Southweft by Weft till ten this night. The fift, was very much wind at North Eafterly : at twelue we ftrooke a Hull, hauing brought our felues neare the mouth of the Inlet.

The fhroudes and fayles frozen.
The mouth of the Inlet.
77. degrees 30. minutes.

The fixth, in the morning the wind was as before, and the Sea growne. This morning we came into a very Greene Sea, we had our obferuation 77. degrees 30. minutes. This after-noone the wind and Sea affwaged. About foure of the clocke we fet fayle, and fteered North-weft and by Weft, the wind being at North North-eaft. This day proued the cleareft day we had long before. The feuenth, at foure in the morning was very cleare weather, and the faireft Morning that we faw in three weekes before, we fteered as afore, being by our account in 78. degrees neareft hand, and out of the *Sacke.* We found we were compaffed in with Land and Ice, and were againe entred into a *Blacke Sea,* which by proofe we found to be an open paffage. Now hauing the wind at North North-eaft, we fteered away South & by Eaft, with purpofe to fall with the Southermoft part of this Land : which we faw, hoping by this meane, either to defray the charge of the Voyage, or elfe, if it pleafed God in time to giue vs a faire wind to the North-eaft, to fatisfie expectation. All this day and night afterward proued calme.

78. degrees.
The end of the Sacke.
A *Blacke* and open Sea.

The eight, all the fore-noone proued calme, and very thicke fogge. This morning we faw many peeces of Drift-wood driue by vs, we heaued out our Boate to ftop a leake, and mended our riggings. This day wee faw many Seales, and two Fifhes which we iudged to bee Sea-horfes, or Morfes. At twelue, this night we had the winde at Eaft and by South, wee ftood away North-eaft.

Much Drift-wood.
Many Seales. Morfes.

The ninth, all the fore-noone was little wind at South-eaft, with thicke fogge. This day we were in amongft Ilands of Ice, where we faw many Seales.

The tenth, in the morning was foggie, afterward it proued cleere, we found we were compaffed with Ice euery way about vs ; wee tacked about, and ftood South and by Weft, and South South-weft one Watch fiue leagues, hoping to get more Sea-roome, and to ftand for the North-eaft, we had the wind at North-weft.

The eleuenth, very cleere weather, with the winde at South South-eaft, we were come out of the *Blue Sea* into our *Greene Sea* againe, where we faw Whales. Now hauing a frefh gale of wind at South South-eaft, it behooued mee to change my courfe, and to fayle to the North-eaft, by the Souther end of *Newland.* But being come into a *Greene Sea,* praying God to direct mee, I fteered away North ten leagues. After that, we faw Ice on our Larboord, we fteered away Eaft and by North three leagues, and left the Ice behind vs. Then we fteered away North till noone. This day wee had the Sunne on the Meridian South and by Weft, his greateft height was 37. degrees 20. minutes. By this obferuation we were in 79. degrees 17. minutes, we had a frefh gale of wind and a fmooth fea, by meanes whereof our fhip had out-runne vs. At ten this Euening cleere weather, and then we had the company of our troublefome neighbours Ice with fogge. The wind was at South South-weft. Heere we faw plentie of Seales, and we fuppofed Beares had beene heere, by their footing and dung vpon the Ice. This day, many of my Companie were ficke with eating of Beares flefh the day before vnfalted.

From hence it feemeth it taken out of Hen. Hudfons owne Notes.
Blue and *Greene Seas.*
79. degrees 17. minutes.
Sick of Beares flefh vnfalted.

The twelfth, for the moft part was thicke fogge, we fteered betweene South and by Eaft, and South South-eaft 2. ½. leagues, to cleere vs of the Ice. Then we had the wind at South, we fteered till noone North-eaft fiue leagues. This morning we had our fhrouds frozen. At noone by our accompt we were in 80. degrees, being little wind at Weft South-weft, almoft calme with thicke fogge. This after-noone we fteered away North, and fometimes North-eaft. Then we faw Ice a head off vs, we caft about an I ftood South-eaft, with little wind and fogge. Before we caft about by meanes of the thicke fogge, we were very neere Ice, being calme, and the Sea fetting on to the Ice, which was very dangerous. It pleafed God at the very inftant to giue vs a fmall gale, which was the meanes of our deliuerance, to him be praife therefore. At twelue this night,

80. degrees.

Newland or
Greenland, of
which the *Hol-*
landers hath
made a little
Difcouerie by
Barents, as be-
fore is deliue-
red, but nei-
ther fo farre,
nor fo exact,
nor fo viefull:
not firft as be-
fore is obfer-
ued of Sir *H.*
Willoughbies
Englifh exacter
Difcoueries
finding the
Whale and
Morfe benefit,
they alfo en-
terloped.
Greene Sea fre-
eft of Ice, and
the *Blue Sea*
Icie.
Collins Cape.
Whale danger?

ıs cleered vp, and out of the top *William Collins* our Boat-fwaine faw the Land, called *Newland*
by the *Hollanders,* bearing South South-weft twelue leagues from vs.

The thirteenth, in the Morning the wind at South and by Eaft, a good gale, we caft about and
ſtood North-eaft and by Eaft, and by obferuation we were in 80. degrees 23. minutes. This day
we faw many Whales. This fore-noone proued cleere weather, and we could not fee any figne of
Ice out of the top. Betweene noone and three of the clocke, we fteered away North-eaft and by
Eaft fiue leagues, then we faw Ice on head off vs, we fteered Eaft two Glaffes one league, and could
not be cleare of the Ice with that courfe. Then we fteered away South-eaft two leagues ½. after
we fayled Eaft and by North, and Eaft foure leagues, till eight the next morning.

10   The foureteenth, in the morning was calme with fogge. At nine the wind at Eaft, a fmall
gale with thicke fogge, we fteered South-eaft and by Eaft, and running this courfe we found
our *Greene Sea* againe, which by proofe we found to be freeft from Ice , and our Azure *Blue Sea*
to be our Icie Sea. At this time we had more Birds then we vfually found. At noone being a
thicke fogge, we found our felues neere Land, bearing Eaft off vs ; and running farther we found
a Bay open to the Weft and by North Northerly, the bottome and fides thereof being to our
fight very high and ragged Land. The Norther fide of this Bayes mouth being high land, is a
fmall Iland, the which we called *Collins* Cape, by the name of our Boat-fwaine, who firft faw it.
In this Bay we faw many Whales, and one of our company hauing a Hooke and Line ouer-boord
to trie for Fifh, a Whale came vnder the Keele of our fhip, and made her held, yet by Gods mer-
20   cie we had no harme, but the loffe of the hooke and three parts of the line. At a South-weft
Sunne from the North-weft and by North, a flood fet into the Bay. At the mouth of this Bay
we had founding thirtie fathoms, and after fixe and twentie fathoms, but being farther in, we
had no ground at an hundred fathoms, and therefore judged it rather a Sound then a Bay. Betweene this high ragged, in the fwampes and vallies lay much fnow. Heere wee found it hot.
On the Souther fide of this Bay, lve three or foure fmall Ilands or Rockes.

A Sound is a
greater and
deeper in-
draught then a
Bay.
Heat beyond
80. degrees.

In the bottome of this Bay, *Iohn Colman* my Mate, and *William Collins* my Boat-fwaine, with
two others of our company went on fhoare, and there they found and brought aboord, a payre of
Morfes teeth in the jaw, they likewife found Whales bones, and fome dofen or more of Deeres
Hornes, they faw the footings of Beafts of other forts, they alfo faw Rote-geefe, they faw much
30   drift Wood on the fhoare, and found a ftreame or two of Frefh water. Here they found it hot on
the fhoare, and dranke water to coole their thirft, which they alfo commended. Here we found
the want of a better Ship-boate. As they certified me, they were not on the fhoare paft halfe an
houre, and among other things brought aboord a Stone of the Countrey. When they went from
vs it was calme, but prefently after we had a gale of wind at North-eaft, which came with the
Flood with fogge. We plyed too and againe in the Bay waiting their comming ; but after they
came aboord we had the wind at Eaft and by South a fine gale, we minding our Voyage, and the
time to performe it, fteered away North-eaft, and North North-eaft. This might proued cleere,
and we had the Sunne on the Meridian, on the North and by Eaft part of the Compaffe, from the
vpper edge of the Horizon with the Croffe-ftaffe, we found his height 10. degrees 40. minutes,
40   without allowing any thing for the Semidiameter of the Sunne, or the diftance of the end of the
ftaffe from the Center in the Eye. From a North Sunne to an Eaft Sunne, we fayled betweene
North and North North-eaft, eight leagues.

Sunne 10. de-
grees 40. min.
high, about
mid-night.

The fifteenth, in the morning was very cleere weather, the Sunne fhining warme, but little
wind at Eaft Southerly. By a South-eaft Sunne we had brought *Collins* Cape to beare off vs
South-eaft, and we faw the high Land of *Newland,* that part by vs Difcouered on our ftarboord,
eight or ten leagues from vs, trending North-eaft and by Eaft, and South-weft and by Weft,
eighteene or twentie leagues from vs to the North-eaft, being a very high Mountaynous land,
like ragged Rockes with fnow betweene them. By mine account, the Norther part of this
Land which now we faw, ftretched into 81. degrees. All this day proued cleere weather, little
Wind, and reafonable warme.

81. degrees.

50   The fixteenth, in the morning warme and cleere weather, the wind at North. This morning
we faw that we were compaffed in with Ice in abundance, lying to the North, to the North-
weft, the Eaft and South-eaft, and being runne toward the fartheft part of the Land by vs difcouered, which for the moft part trendeth neareft hand North-eaft and South-weft, we faw
more Land ioyning to the fame, trending North in our fight, by meanes of the cleerneffe of the
weather, ftretching farre into 82. degrees ; and by the bowing or fhewing of the skie much farther. Which when I firft faw, I hoped to haue had a free Sea betweene the Land and the Ice, and
meant to haue compaffed this Land by the North. But now finding by proofe it was vnpoffible,
by meanes of the abundance of Ice compaffing vs about by the North, and ioyning to the land, and
feeing God did bleffe vs with a faire wind to fayle by the South of this Land to the North-eaft,
60   we returned, bearing vp the Helme, minding to hold that part of the Land, which the *Hollan-*
ders had difcouered in our fight, and if contrary windes fhould take vs, to Harbour there, and to
trie what we could finde to the charge of our Voyage, and to proceed on our Difcouerie, as foone
as God fhould bleffe vs with Winde. And this I can affure at this prefent, that betweene 78. degrees

Land ftretch-
ing into 82. de-
grees.

They returned

grees and ¼. and 82. degrees by this way there is no paſſage : but I thinke this Land may bee
profitable to thoſe that will aduenture it. In this Bay before ſpoken of, and about this coaſt, we

Abundance of Seales. ſaw more abundance of Seales then we had ſeene any time before ſwimming in the water. At
noone, this day hauing a ſtiffe gale of wind at North, we were thwart of *Collins* Cape, ſtanding
in 81. degrees and a halfe : and at one of the clocke the Cape beare North-eaſt off vs. From
thence I ſet our courſe Weſt South-weſt , with purpoſe to keepe in the open Sea free from
Ice, and ſayled in that courſe 16. leagues. At ten this night we ſteered away South-weſt, with
the wind at North a hard gale, vntill eight the next morning 18. leagues.

The ſeuenteenth, in the morning a good gale at North : at eight, we altered our courſe, and
ſteered away South till eight in the Eeuening, and ranne 12. leagues. This day proued reaſona- 10
ble cleere and warme. The eighteenth, in the morning the wind encreaſed at South and by
Eaſt, with thicke fogge. All this after-noone and night proued cloſe weather, little fogge, and
reaſonable warme.

The nineteenth, at eight in the morning the wind at South, with thicke fogge, we ſteered
South-eaſt 4. leagues till noone : then the wind vered more large ; wee ſteered South-eaſt and
by Eaſt 4. leagues till foure : then wee vered ſhete , and ſteered Eaſt and by South Eaſterly,
15. leagues, till eight the next morning. This day after the morning proued reaſonable cleere
and warme.

The twentieth, in the morning little wind : at eight this morning wee ſaw Land ahead of
vs vnder our Lee, and to weatherward of vs diſtant from vs 12. leagues, being part of *New-* 20
land. It is very high mountainous Land ; the higheſt that we had ſeene vntill now. As we ſayled neere it, we ſaw a Sound ahead of vs, lying Eaſt and weſt. The Land on the Norther ſide
of this Sounds mouth, trendeth neereſt hand Weſt North-weſt, and Eaſt South-eaſt 12. leagues,
in our ſight being 10. leagues from vs. And the Land on the Souther ſide being 8. or 10. leagues
in our ſight; at this time trendeth South South-eaſt, and North North-weſt; from eight to noone
77. degr. 26. m. was calme. This day by obſeruation we were in 77. degrees 26. minutes. On the Norther ſide
of the mouth of this Inlet lie three Ilands, not farre the one from the other , being very high
mountainous Land. The fartheſt of the three to the North-weſt, hath foure very high Mounts
like heapes of Corne. That Iland next the Inlets mouth, hath one very high Mount on the
Souther end. Here one of our companie killed a red billed Bird. All this day after the mor- 30
ning, and all night proued calme, enclining rather to heate then cold. This night wee had ſome
warme rayne.

The one and twentieth, all the fore-noone calme ; at foure in the after-noone we had a ſmall
gale of wind at South South-eaſt, with fog ; we ſteered away Eaſt to ſtand in with the Land,
and ſayled 3. leagues vntill mid-night : then the wind came at North-eaſt, we caſt about, and
ſteered South 10. leagues till eight the next morning. The two and twentieth, at eight in the
morning much wind at Eaſt, and variable, with ſhort ſayle wee ſteered 3. leagues South and by
Eaſt : then came downe very much wind ; wee ſtrooke a hull. All this after-noone and night,
proued very much wind with raine.

The three and twentieth , all the fore-noone was very much wind at South, with raine and 40
fogge. At foure this after-poone wee ſaw Land , bearing North-eaſt of vs 6. leagues from vs.
Then we had the wind at South South-weſt ; wee ſteered away South-eaſt, and South-eaſt and
by Eaſt 4. leagues, the Sea being very much growne. We accounted we had hulled North-weſt
and by North 22. leagues ; and North 3. leagues. Then fearing with much wind to be ſet on a
lee ſhoare, we tackt about, and made our way good Weſt and by North, halfe a point Northerly,
all this night with much wind.

The foure and twentieth , in the morning much wind as afore, and the Sea growne. This
morning wee ſtrooke our mayne Top-maſt to eaſe our ſhip, and ſayled from the laſt Eeuening
eight to this noone 15. leagues Weſt and by North halfe a point Northerly. From twelue to
eight, 6. leagues as afore, with the wind at South and by Weſt : at eight we tackt about with 50
the winde at South South-weſt, and lay South-eaſt and by Eaſt, with much winde, and the
Sea growne.

The fiue and twentieth, was a cleere morning we ſet our mayne Top-maſt, we ſaw Land bearing North of vs, and vnder our Lee, we ſayling South-eaſt and by Eaſt. Then the wind ſcanted:
we caſt about, and lay South-weſt and by Weſt 2. leagues ⅓ till noone. Then it began to ouer-caſt,
and the wind to ſcant againe: we caſt about, and lay South-eaſt and by South, the wind at South-
weſt and by Weſt, and ſayled in that courſe 3. leagues till foure in the after-noone. Then the
wind ſcanted againe, and we ſayled 3. leagues South. Now, ſeeing how contrarie the winde
proued , to doe the good which wee deſired this way ; I thought to proue our fortunes by the
Weſt once againe: and this Eeuening at eight, wee being the latitude of 78. with the better, 60
and from Land 15. leagues , which leagues part whereof beare from the North-eaſt to the Eaſt
off vs, we ſteered away Weſt, with the wind at South-eaſt, and cleere weather.

The ſixe and twentieth, all this day proued rayne with thicke fog, and an hard gale of wind
at Eaſt and by North, and Eaſt North-eaſt. From the laſt Eeuening at eight to this noone, wee

ranne

ranne 25. leagues : from noone till mid-night 19. leagues, the wind at Eaſt and by South ; from mid-night till two the next morning, 2. leagues Weſt.

The ſeuen and twentieth, extreme thicke fog, and little wind at Eaſt and by South. Then it proued calme, and the Sea very loftie. Wee heard a great rutte or noiſe with the Ice and Sea, which was the firſt Ice we heard or ſaw ſince we were at *Collins* Cape: the Sea heauing vs Weſt-ward toward the Ice. Wee heaued out our Boat, and rowed to towe out our ſhip farther from the danger ; which would haue beene to ſmall purpoſe, by meanes the Sea went ſo high : but in this extremitie it pleaſed God to giue vs a ſmall gale at North-weſt and by Weſt, we ſteered a-way South-eaſt 4. leagues till noone. Here we had finiſhed our Diſcouerie, if the wind had con- *Danger eſca-*

10 tinued that brought vs hither , or if it had continued calme: but it pleaſed God to make this *ped.* North-weſt, and by Weſt wind the meane of our deliuerance : which wind wee had not found common in this Voyage. God giue vs thankfull hearts for ſo great deliuerance. Here we found *Whales Bay,* the want of a good ſhip-boat, as once we had done before at *Whales Bay :* we wanted alſo halfe a dozen long Oares to rowe in our ſhip. At noone the day cleered vp, and we ſaw by the skie Ice bearing off vs: from Weſt South-weſt to the North and North North-eaſt. Then we had a good gale at Weſt, we ſteered away South till foure 7. leagues. From foure to ſix South 4. leagues, and found by the Icy skie and our neereneſſe to *Groneland,* that there is no paſſage that way : which if there had beene, I meant to haue made my returne by the North of *Groneland* to *Dauis* his Streights, and ſo for *England.* Here finding we had the benefit of a Weſterly wind , which

20 all this Voyage we had found ſcant, we altered our courſe, and ſteered to the Eaſtward , and ran South-eaſt foure leagues. From eight this Eeuening till noone the next day ; Eaſt South-eaſt 30. leagues. All this day and night proued very cold, by meanes, as I ſuppoſe, of the winds com-ming off ſo much Ice.

The eight and twentieth, very cold, the wind at Weſt, not very foggie. At noone this day we ſteered away South-eaſt and by Eaſt, and by obſeruation we were 76. degrees 36. minutes. From noone to eight 10. leagues. Then the wind ſcanted to South-eaſt and by South , we ſtee-red away Eaſt and by North 18. leagues, till the next day noone.

The nine and twentieth, all the fore-noone a thicke fog and wet, the wind at South-eaſt and by Eaſt, neereſt hand, and raw cold. From noone to foure, wee ſayled three leagues Eaſt and by

30 North, halfe a point Northerly.Then the wind vered more large, we ſteered Eaſt and by South 8. leagues till twelue at night. At this timet to windward we heard the rutte of Land ; which I knew to be ſo, by the colour of the Sea. It was extreme thicke fog, ſo that we could hardly ſee a Cables length from our ſhip. We had ground 25. fathoms, ſmall blacke peble ſtones. Wee ſounded againe , and had ground at 30. fathomes ſmall ſtones like Beanes , at the next caſt no ground at 60. fathomes. I caſt about againe , and ſteered South-weſt 6. leagues, Weſt and by North two leagues till the next day noone. All this day and night extreme thicke fog.

The thirtieth, all the fore-noone very thicke fog. At noone almoſt calme : after we had little wind, and ſteered North North-weſt till two : then it cleered vp, ſo that we could ſee from vs 2. leagues with the wind at North-weſt.Then we ſteered Eaſt South-eaſt: after it cleered. At

40 South in the Eeuening, we ſaw an Iland bearing off vs North-weſt from vs 5. leagues, and we ſaw land bearing off vs from vs 7. leagues.We had land likewiſe bearing off vs from Eaſt South-eaſt , to South-eaſt and by Eaſt as wee iudged , 10. leagues. Then hauing the winde at Weſt North-weſt,we ſteered South and by Eaſt. It preſently proued calme till ten this Eeuening : then wee had a little gale at South-weſt and by Weſt, wee ſteered away South South-eaſt till twelue this night, and accounted ourſelues in 76. from Land 10. leagues: which was the like-lieſt Land that wee had ſeene on all the parts of *Newland,* being playne riggie Land of a meane height,and not ragged as all the reſt was that we had ſeene this Voyage, nor couered with ſnow. At twelue this night we ſaw two Morſes in the Sea neere vs, ſwimming to Land. From twelue at night to foure, calme.

50 The one and thirtieth, at foure this morning we had the wind at South-eaſt, we ſteered South South-weſt. Then it proued calme, and ſo continued all the fore-noone. The after-noone wee had the wind at Eaſt South-eaſt , we ſteered South 8. leagues. Then being like to proue much wind,contrarie to our purpoſe, and finding our fog more thicke and troubleſome then before, di-uers things neceſſarie wanting, and our time well nigh ſpent to doe further good this yeere , I commanded to beare vp for our returne for *England,* and ſteered away South South-weſt. And this night proued a hard gale of wind at South-eaſt and by Eaſt. Wee were thwart of *Cheries* *Cherie Iland.* Iland the next morning at foure of the clocke, being to windward off vs 5. leagues : knowing we were neere it, we looked out carefully for the ſame, and it prouing cleere, we ſaw it , being a very ragged Land on the Weſter ſide, riſing like Hey-cockes.

60 The firſt of Auguſt, a very hard gale of wind at Eaſt South-eaſt, we ſhorted ſayle, and ſteered away South South-weſt. This night was very foggie, with a hard gale of wind at Eaſt and by South, we ſteered by our account 27. leagues : and from eight this Eeuening till the next mor-ning foure, 10. leagues as afore. All this night was very foggie, wet and raw cold.

The ſecond, in the morning calme with a thicke fog, cold and ſlabbie weather. About noone

we

we had a little gale West and by North, wee steered away as afore. The third, in the morning calme and cleere weather, with a little gale East and by South, we sayled South South-west: then wee had the wind at South-east, wee sayled as afore. All this day and night proued close weather, a little fogge at noone, which continued not long. At twelue this night the wind vered to the East and by North, wee held our course South South-west, as afore.

The fifteenth of August, we put into the Iles of *Farre*, standing in 52. degrees; and the fif-teenth of September, I arriued in *Tilberie Hope* in the *Thames.*

C H A P. XV.

10

A second Voyage or Employment of Master H E N R Y H V D S O N, *for finding
a passage to the East* Indies *by the North-east:
written by himselfe.*

[note] I haue *Robert
Iuets* Iournall
also, for breui-
tie omitted.

Heir names employed in this action are as followeth: *Henry Hudson*, Master and Pilot; *Robert* [note] *Iuet*, the Master his Mate; *Ludlowe Arnall*; *Iohn Cooke*, Boat-sonne; *Philip Stacie*, Carpenter; *Iohn Barns*; *Iohn Braunch*, Cooke; *Iohn A-drey*, *Iames Strutton*, *Michael Feirce*, *Thomas Hilles*, *Richard Tomson*, *Ro-bert Raynar*, *Iohn Hudson*, and *Humfrey Gilby*. The courses obserued in this Iournall were by a Compasse, that the Needle and the North of the Flye were directly one on the other.

20

Aprill.

Anno 1608. the two and twentieth of Aprill, being Friday, we set sayle at Saint *Katherines,* and fell downe to *Blacke wall.*

May.

The twentieth of May, at noone by obseruation we were in 64. degrees 52. minutes, and at this time and place the Needle declined vnder the Horizon by the Inclinatory 81. degrees, and wee had a smooth Sea, by meanes whereof my obseruation was good.

The one and twentieth, at night thicke fog, wee sayled North North-east, with the wind at East. The two and twentieth, in the fore-noone the winde at South-east, wee steered North North-east, as afore: in the after-noone little wind and thicke fog; we accounted vs in 67. de- 30 grees, the Sea smooth, the Needle declined 82. degrees, this night was calme and cleere. The three and twentieth, in the morning the wind was Easterly, we stood North North-East, and North and by East. All the fore-noone was foggie: in the after-noone it cleered, and the wind shortned vpon vs, we made our way good North all night. The foure and twentieth, the wind at East North-east, and East and by North, we lay as neere as wee could with a full sayle; wee

Lowfoe.

accounted *Lowfoot* from vs East Northerly, 16. leagues, distant from vs; at foure a clocke this after-noone, wee stood all night, as afore.

The fiue and twentieth, the wind at East North-east, we stood away North as we could lie: all this day was cleere weather, and searching cold, which cold begunne the one and twentieth day, and then my Carpenter was taken sicke, and so doth yet continue; and three or foure more 40 of our companie were enclining to sicknesse, I suppose by meanes of the cold. All the night it was calme. The sixe and twentieth, cold but cleere weather, the wind betweene East and East North-east, we stood North-easterly till twelue a clocke at night: then wee had the wind at North-east & North North-east, we stood South-east and East till noone the next day. The seuen and twentieth, cold and drie weather, at noone we had the wind North and North North-west; Wee stood away North-east, and East North-east, as we could, and accounted our selues in 69. degrees 40. minutes, and the Needle enclined, hauing a smooth Sea, neerest 84. degrees. All night we had wind and weather as afore.

The eight and twentieth, drie cold cleere weather; the wind betweene North North-west

**Sun 5. degrees
35. minutes at
mid-night.**

and North, we made our way good East North-east; wee saw the Sunne on the North Meri- 50 dian aboue the Horizon 5. degrees 35. minutes. All this night we had much wind, as afore. The nine and twentieth, a hard gale at North North-west: by account we ranne from mid-night to noone 21. leagues, East North-east. Wee had the Sunne on the Meridian 5. degrees, the lati-tude 73. degrees 13. minutes, whereby wee found our ship to haue out-runne vs. At mid-night the wind came to South-east: we cast about, and stood East North-east. This day partly cleere weather with some snow. The thirtieth, cold cleere weather, the wind betweene North-east, and East and by North; we went East South-east, and obseruing, were in 73. degrees 50. mi-nutes. The one and thirtieth, cold and cleere weather: from the last day till this day noone, we stood South-east and by South, in the latitude of 72. degrees 45. minutes.

Iune.

The first of Iune, a hard gale at East North-East, with snow: we made our way good South 60 South-east. The second, a hard gale of wind at North-east: towards night, calme with fogge,

North Cape.

our course was South-east all day. The third, in the morning we had a sight of the North Cape;

**Variation west
11. degrees.**

and at a West and by North Sunne, the Cape bore off vs South-west, halfe a point Southerly, being from vs 8. leagues: and obseruing the variation, I found it to the Westward 11. degrees:

and

and hauing a smooth Sea, the Needle enclined vnder the Horizon 84. degrees and a halfe, the neerest I could finde. We had the wind at South-west, and wee stood away North-east and by East. It was cleere weather, and we saw *Norway* Fisher-men at Sea. **Needles inclination 84. degrees and a halfe.**

The fourth, warme cleere sun-shine, we stood away North-east and by East. Now by Gods helpe our Carpenter recouered, and made a Mast for our ship-boat, and the companie made a Sayle, we had the Sunne in the sight on the North Meridian: his height was 5. degrees 40. minutes. Inclination 23.degrees 21. minutes: Poles height 72. degrees 21. minutes. The fift, in the morning calme weather: wee sounded, and had 140. fathoms, sand Oze: here wee saw a swelling Sea setting North-east and by East, and South-west and by West, with streame-leches: and we saw drift wood. After we had wind; and we sayled and made our way North North-east: towards night we sounded, and found ground at 150. fathoms, sand Oze. This day cleere weather, and not cold. The sixt, wee had cleere weather, the wind being at East North-East, from the last day till this day noone; we shaped our way on diuers courses North and by West, in the latitude of 73. degrees 24. minutes. We found that our ship had out-runne vs, sounding in 160. fathoms: in the after-noone little wind.

The seuenth, in the morning the wind at South, after at South South-east: from the last day till this day noone, wee accounted our way from diuers courses North-east, 15. leagues. This day was close but cleere weather, and we had a good gale of wind at this time. And three dayes before this, our Cooke and one more of our companie were very sicke. In the morning, we had ground at 150. fathoms, and at night we had no ground at 180. fathoms, which encreased hope. This night we had some snow, which continued foure houres: then the wind came at North-east and by East with storme; and with short sayle we stood North and by West: here the Needle enclined 86. degrees. I accounted that we were in 74. degrees and a halfe at neerest hand. This night we saw the Sunne on the North Meridian, his height was 7. degrees 40. minutes, which maketh the Poles height 74. degrees 23. minutes. The eight, from twelue a clocke last night till noone, we accounted our way on diuers courses, North and by East: then our latitude was 74. degrees 38. minutes, and we had no ground at 200. fathoms. In the after-noone the wind came at South South-east, and South-east and by East. This day and night wee had cleere weather, and we were here come into a blacke blue Sea. **74. degrees 30. minutes.**

Darke blue Sea.

The ninth, cleere weather, the wind came at South-east and by East: from the last day till this day noone, wee had a good way North-east, in latitude of 75. degrees 29. minutes: then wee entred into Ice, being the first we saw in this Voyage: our hope was to goe through it, we stood into it, and held our course betweene North-east, and East North-east, loosing for one, and bearing roome for another, till foure in the after-noone: at which time we were so farre in, and the Ice so thicke and firme ahead, being in it foure or fiue leagues, that wee had endangered vs somewhat too farre; wee returned as wee went in, and with a few rubbes of our ship against the Ice; by eight a clocke this Euening wee got free of it. Wee made our way till next day at noone, South-west and by South, 18. leagues: in the middest of this way wee had no ground at 180. fathoms. The tenth, in the morning hasey weather; but at noone it cleered vp, and then we cast about, and stood away North and by East, the wind being at East South-east, two watches, fiue leagues: then we had the wind at East, we cast about, and stood South South-east, and made a South way, sixe leagues. The eleuenth, in the morning a hard storme at East, and East and by South we strooke ahull.

The twelfth, in the morning fog, and all day after cleere weather, the wind at South South-west, we steered East and by North: at noone being in the latitude 75.degrees 30.minutes. From noone till foure a clocke, fiue leagues East and by North; then we saw Ice ahead of vs, and vnder our Lee trending from the North-west to the North and East of vs: We had sounding 100. fathom, greenish Oze. Here we saw diuers pieces of drift wood by vs driuing, and streame Leeches lying South South-west, and North North-east. We many times saw the like since we saw the North Cape. The thirteenth, cleere weather, the wind at East, we made a South way 6.leagues, two watches: then we cast about, and made a North way one watch 3. leagues ¼: At twelue at night, much wind with fog, we strooke ahull and layed our ships head to the Southward. The fourteenth, in the fore-noone fog, and our shroudes were frozen: the after-noone was cleere Sun-shine, and so was all the night.

The fifteenth, all day and night cleere sun-shine; the wind at East, the latitude at noone 75. degrees 7. minutes. We held Westward by our account 13. leagues. In the after-noone the Sea was asswaged; and the wind being at East we set sayle, and stood South and by East, and South South-east as we could. This morning, one of our companie looking ouer boord saw a Mermaid, and calling vp some of the companie to see her, one more came vp, and by that time shee was come close to the ships side, looking earnestly on the men: a little after, a Sea came and ouerturned her: from the Nauill vpward, her backe and breasts were like a womans, (as they say that saw her) her body as big as one of vs; her skin very white; and long haire hanging downe behind, of colour blacke: in her going downe they saw her tayle, which was like the tayle of a Porposse, and speckled like a Macrell. Their names that saw her, were *Thomas Hilles* and *Robert Rayner*. **Mermaide seene, and described.**

The

The sixteenth, cleere weather, the wind being at East. From the last day till this day noone, we made our way South and by East 9. leagues; and from noon to eight a clocke in the Eeuening, 6. leagues : then we cast about and stood to the Northwards.

The seuenteenth, cleere weather, the wind at South-east and by East; from the last day till this day noone,our way was North-east and by East,at noone being in the latitude of 74.degrees 40. minutes. At after-noone we sounded,and had ground at 86.fathom,greene Oze,and our water whitish greene : Here we saw Whales, Porpoises, and the Sea full of Fowles : from noone to mid-night North-east and by East we had the Sunne at lowest , on the North and by East, Easterly part of the Compasse : latitude 74. degrees 54. minutes. Sounding we had 92. fathoms water, Oze as before.   10

The eighteenth, faire weather, the wind at South-east and by East,from mid-night till this day noone, wee sayled North-east and by East, in the Latitude of 75. degrees 24. minutes, and had ground at ninetie fiue fathome Oze, as afore. Heere we had Ice in our sight to the Northward off vs. In the after-noone, hauing little wind at North-east, we cast about and lay East South-east, and at sixe a clocke, had ground at ninetie fiue fathoms and a halfe Oze, as afore. From noone to twelue a clocke at night, our way was South-east, and South-east and by East, and had the Sunne on the Meridian, North and by East halfe a point Eastward. The Sunnes

Current. height was eight degrees 40.minutes. Sounding ninetie fathom. All this day, we had Ice on our Larboord trending : and at this time,from the North-west off vs to the East South-east, I haue some reason to thinke there is a Tide or Current setting to the Northwards ; the course wee held and the way we made betweene this noone and mid-night Obseruations, doe make mee suspect it the more.   20

Needles inclination 89.de-grees and a halfe, in 75.de-grees 22.min. The nineteenth,faire and warme weather,the sea smooth. Here the Needle inclined vnder the Horizon 89. degrees and a halfe,being in the Latitude at noone of 75.degrees 22.minutes; Sounding wee had ground in an hundred fathom. From twelue a clocke last night till this day at noone, we accounted our way from East and by North to South-east,ten leagues, hauing Ice alwayes in our sight trending on our Larboord, wee had the winde betweene North, and North North-west. We saw the Sunne at the lowest on the North and by East,halfe a point Easterly, his height was 8. degrees 10. minutes, which maketh the Poles height 74. degrees 56. minutes; Sounding we had ground in one hundred and twentie sixe fathom. From noone to this time,wee accounted our way East and by South, and East South-east, twelue leagues.   30

Beares roaring Store of Seals. The twentieth, faire warme weather, this morning at foure of the clocke,wee had depth one hundred and twentie fiue fathom. Heere we heard Beares roare on the Ice ; and we saw vpon the Ice and neare vnto it, an incredible number of Seales. We had sounding one hundred and fifteen fathom,and after ground at ninetie fiue fathoms andie Oze. We had the Sun on the Meridian North and by East, halfe a point Easterly ; his height was 7. degrees 20. minutes. From twelue a clocke last night, to twelue a clocke this night, our way was made good by our account South-east and by South,twelue leagues, and South-east ,three leagues and a halfe, the Ice alwayes being on our Larboord. The wind this day, betweene North and North-west.

The one and twentieth, at foure a clocke in the morning wee sounded, and had one hundred 40 and twentie fathome greene Oze, and the Ice bore off vs East, the winde variable ; in diuers courses wee made our way good South South-east; our Latitude at noone being 74. degrees 9.

Sunne at mid-night high 7. degrees 40.minutes, in 74. degrees 33.minutes. Iuets notes tell of a sudden variation of the Compasse, from the North to the East one point, which had been two imediately before. minutes, we were haled to the Northward beyond expectation. All this day faire, cleere,and warme weather, and Ice on our Larboord at a North and by East Sunne ; being then at lowest, his height was 7.degrees 40. minutes, which made the Poles height 74. degrees 33. minutes. From the last day at noone, till twelue a clocke this night, by account of our ships way, wee made our way good East North-east, sixe leagues and a halfe ; whereby it doth appeare how we were haled to the Northward. Heere wee had ground at one hundred and thirteene fathome, greene sandie Oze.

The two and twentieth, faire cleare weather, the winde at West North-west. At eight a 50 clocke in the Morning, we had ground at one hundred and fifteene fathom, greene Oze. From mid-night to noone, our course was North-east and by East, being in the Latitude of 74. degrees 35.minutes, and we found that our ships way, and our obseruation were not   but there was carefull heed taken of both. Heere we had Ice a head off vs, trending to the South-east ; and all day before Ice on our Larboord. Here we stood South-east fiue leagues, then the Ice trended South and by West sixe leagues ; we sayled by it, and doubled it by eight a clocke in the Eeuening, and then it bore East off vs. Heere hauing a smooth sea, the Needle inclined 85. degrees,from eight a clocke to twelue,North and by East Easterly. Then we had the Sunne on the Meridian, North and by East ½. a poynt Easterly. The Sunnes height was 7.degrees 45.minutes, which made the Latitude 74.degrees 43.minutes.

The three and twentieth,in the morning thicke fogge, the wind at North North-west. From 60 mid-night till foure a clocke this morning, we sayled North-east fiue leagues, and then we were among the Ice ; we cast about,and stood two houres South-west,two leagues, and had no ground at one hundred and eightie fathom. Then we cast about againe, and stood East till eight a clocke

two

two leagues, and then it cleered vp, and we had Ice a head off vs. And from North, we stood to South-east, and our shroudes were frozen. Then till noone, wee went East and by South, foure leagues, and were neere Ice on our Larboord, in the Latitude of 74. degrees 30. minutes. In the after-noone the wind being at North, wee stood two houres and a halfe, fiue leagues and a halfe; three houres South South-east, fiue leagues; one houre South-east and by South, one league and a halfe; an houre East halfe a league, which brought eight in the Eeuening alwayes Ice on our Larboord. This after-noone, wee had some snow. From eight a clocke to mid-night, South South-west foure leagues, with Ice as afore. We saw the Sunne at the lowest, North North-east, his height was 7. degrees 15. minutes, the Poles height 74. degrees 18. minutes.

10   The foure and twentieth, cleere, but cold and some snow, the wind betweene North North-east, and North-east, from mid-night to foure a clocke, wee stood Southward two leagues, and South-east and by East two leagues. And from foure a clocke till noone, South-east Southerly nine leagues, sounding we had ground in one hundred and fortie fathome. From noone to three a clocke, we stood South-east and by South three leagues; from three to foure, South-west and by South one league; and had Ice from the North-east to the South-east off vs. From foure a clocke to eight, we stood South-west two leagues and a halfe, Southward halfe a league, with Ice neere vs vnder our Lead.

The fiue and twentieth, cold and cleare, the wind at East South-east; from eight a clocke last night till foure this morning, our way was South and by East, foure leagues and a halfe; soun-
20 ding we had ground in eightie fathome, then we had little wind till noone, at East North-east, and the Sunne on the Meridian, on the South-west and by South point of the Compasse, ere it began to fall, wee were in the Latitude of 72. degrees 52. minutes, and had Ice on our Larboord, and our hope of passage was gone this way, by meanes of our nearenesse to *Noua Zembla,* and the abundance of Ice. We had from Noone to eight a clocke in the Eeuening, the wind betweene North North-east, and North-east, we stood South-east three leagues and a halfe, and had Ice on our Larboord, and shoalding sixtie eight fathome.

The sixe and twentieth, faire Sun-shining weather, and little wind at East North-east. From twelue a clocke at night till foure this morning, we stood Southward two leagues, sounding wee had sixtie sixe fathome Ooze, as afore. From foure a clocke to noone, South-east and by South
30 foure leagues, and had the Sunne on the Meridian, on the South-east and by South point of the Compasse, in the Latitude of 72. degrees 25. minutes, and had sight of *Noua Zembla* foure or fiue leagues from vs, and the place called by the *Hollanders,* Swart *Cliffe,* bearing off South-east. In the after-noone, wee had a fine gale at East North-east, and by eight of the clocke, we had brought it to beare off vs East Southerly, and sayled by the shoare a league from it. No passage that way. Swart Cliffe

The seuen and twentieth, all the fore-noone it was almost calme; wee being two mile from the shoare, I sent my Mate *Robert Inet,* and *Iohn Cooke* my Boat-swaine on shoare, with foure o-thers, to see what the Land would yeeld that might bee profitable, and to fill two or three Caskes with water. They found and brought aboord some Whales Finnes, two Deeres Hornes, and the Dung of Deere, and they told me that they saw Grasse on the shoare of the last yeere, They goe on shoare.
40 and young Grasse came vp amongst it a shaftman long; and it was boggie ground in some pla-ces, there are many streames of Snow water nigh, it was very hot on the shoare, and the snow melted apace, they saw the footings of many great Beares, of Deere, and Foxes. They went from vs at three a clocke in the morning, and came aboord at a South-east Sunne; and at their comming, wee saw two or three companies of Morses in the sea neere vs swimming, being al-most calme. I presently sent my Mate, *Ladlow* the Carpenter, and sixe others a shoare, to a place where I thought the Morses might come on the shoare, they found the place likely, but found no signe of any that had beene there. There was a Crosse standing on the shoare, much Drift-wood, and signes of Fires that had beene made there. They saw the footing of very great Deere and Beares, and much Fowle, and a Foxe; they brought aboord Whale finnes, some Mosse, Flow-
50 ers and greene things that did there grow. They brought also two peeces of a Crosse, which they found there. The Sunne was on the Meridian on the North North-east, halfe a point Ea-sterly, before it began to fall. The Sunnes height was 4. degrees 45. minutes, Inclination 22. degrees 33. minutes, which makes the Latitude 72. degrees 12. minutes. There is disagree-ment betweene this and the last obseruation; but by meanes of the cleerenesse of the Sunne, the smoothnesse of the Sea, and the neernesse to Land, wee could not bee deceiued, and care was taken in it.

The eight and twentieth, at foure a clocke in the Morning our Boat came aboord, and brought two dozen of Fowle, and some Egges, whereof a few were good, and a Whales finne; and wee all saw the Sea full of Morses, yet no signes of their being on shoare. And in this calme, from
60 eight a clocke last Eeuening, till foure this Morning, we were drawne backe to the Northward, as farre as wee were the last Eeuening at foure a clocke, by a Streame or a Tide; and we chose ra-ther so to driue, then to aduenture the losse of an Anchor, and the spoyle of a Cable. Heere our new Ship-boate began to doe vs seruice, and was an incouragement to my Companie, which want I found the last yeere.

The

The nine and twentieth, in the morning calme, being halfe a league from the fhoare, the Sea being fmooth, the Needle did encline 84. degrees, we had many Morfes in the Sea neere vs, and defiring to find where they came on fhoare, wee put to with Sayle and Oares, towing in our Boat, and rowing in our Barke to get about a point of Land, from whence the Land did fall more Eafterly, and the Morfes did goe that way. VVee had the Sunne on the Meridian on the South and by VVeft point, halfe a point to the VVefter part of the Compaffe, in the latitude of 71. degrees 15. minutes. At two a clocke this after-noone we came to anchor in the mouth of a

Riuer and Iland.

Riuer, where lieth an Iland in the mouth thereof, foure leagues: wee anchored from the Iland in two and thirtie fathomes, blacke fandy ground. There droue much Ice out of it with a ftreame that fet out of the Riuer or Sound, and there were many Morfes fleeping on the Ice, 10 and by it we were put from our Road twice this night; and being calme all this day, it pleafed God at our need to giue vs a fine gale, which freed vs out of danger. This day was calme, cleere and hot weather: all the night we rode ftill.

The thirtieth, calme, hot, and faire weather, we weighed in the morning, and towed and rowed, and at noone we came to anchor neere the Ile aforefaid in the mouth of the Riuer, and faw very much Ice driuing in the Sea, two leagues without vs lying South-eaft and North-weft; and driuing to the North-weft fo faft, that wee could not by twelue a clocke at night fee it out of the top. At the Iland where wee rode, lieth a little Rocke, whereon were fortie or fiftie Morfes lying afleepe, being all that it could hold, it being fo full and little. I fent my companie afhoare to them, leauing none abord but my Boy with mee: and by meanes of their neereneffe 20 to the water, they all got away, faue one which they killed, and brought his head abord; and ere they came abord they went on the Iland, which is reafonable high and fteepe, but flat on the top. They killed and brought with them a great Fowle, whereof there were many, and likewife fome Egges, and in an houre they came abord. This Ile is two flight-fhot ouer in length, and one in breadth. At mid-night our Anchor came home, and wee tayld aground by meanes of the ftrength of the ftreame, but by the helpe of God, wee houed her off without hurt. In fhort time wee moued our fhip, and rode ftill all night; and in the night wee had little wind at Eaft, and Eaft South-eaft. VVee had at noone this day an obferuation, and were in the latitude of 71. degrees 15. minutes.

Iuly.

The firft of Iuly, we faw more Ice to Seaward of vs; from the South-eaft to the North-weft, 30 driuing to the North-weft. At noone it was calme, and we had the Sunne on the Meridian, on the South and by VVeft point, halfe a point to the VVefterly part of the Compaffe, in the latitude of 71. degrees 24. minutes. This morning I fent my Mate *Eueret*, and foure of our companie to rowe about the Bay, to fee what Riuers were in the fame, and to find where the Morfes did come on land; and to fee a Sound or great Riuer in the bottome of the Bay, which did alwaies fend out a great ftreame to the Northwards, againft the tide that came from thence: and I found the fame in comming in, from the North to this place before this. VVhen by the meanes of the great plenty of Ice, the hope of paffage betweene *Newland* and *Noua Zembla* was ta-

His purpofe altered.

ken away; my purpofe was by the *Vaygats* to paffe by the mouth of the Riuer *Ob*, and to double 40 that way the North Cape of *Tartaria*, or to giue reafon wherefore it will not be: but being here, and hoping by the plentie of Morfes wee faw here, to defray the charge of our Voyage; and alfo that this Sound might for fome reafons bee a better paffage to the Eaft of *Noua Zembla*, then the *Vaygats*, if it held according to my hope conceiued by the likeneffe it gaue: for whereas we had a floud came from the Northwards; yet this Sound or Riuer did runne fo ftrong, that

Strong ftream.

Ice with the ftreame of this Riuer was carried away, or any thing elfe againft the floud: fo that both in floud and ebbe, the ftreame doth hold a ftrong courfe; and it floweth from the North three houres, and ebbeth nine.

The fecond, the wind being at Eaft South-eaft, it was reafonable cold, and fo was Friday; and the Morfes did not play in our fight as in warme weather. This morning at three of the clocke, my Mate and companie came abord, and brought a great Deeres horne, a white locke of 50 Deeres haire; foure dozen of Fowle, their Boat halfe laden with drift Wood; and fome Flowers

Herd of white Deere.

and greene things, that they found growing on the fhoare. They faw a herd of white Deere, of ten in a companie on the land; much drift wood lying on the fhoare, many good Bayes, and one Riuer faire to fee to on the North fhoare, for the Morfes to land on: but they faw no Morfes there, but fignes that they had beene in the Bayes. And the great Riuer or Sound, they certified me, was of breadth two or three leagues, and had no ground at twentie fathoms, and that the water was of the colour of the Sea, and very falt, and that the ftreame fetteth ftrongly out of it. At fixe a clocke this morning, came much Ice from the Southward driuing vpon vs, very fearefull to looke on: but by the mercy of God and his mightie helpe, wee being moored with two Anchors ahead with vering out of one Cable, and heauing home the other, and fen- 60 ding off with Beames and Sparres, efcaped the danger: which labour continued till fixe a clocke in the Eeuening, and then it was paft vs, and we rode ftill and tooke our reft this night.

The third, the wind at North a hard gale: At three a clocke this morning wee weighed our anchor, and fet fayle, purpofing to runne into the Riuer or Sound before fpoken of.

The

The fourth, in the morning it cleered vp with the wind at North-weft, we weighed and fet fayle, and ftood to the Eaftwards, and paft ouer a Reefe, and found on it fiue and a halfe, fixe, fixe an a halfe, and feuen fathoms water: then we faw that the Sound was full,& a very large Riuer from the North-eaftward free from Ice, and a ftrong ftreame comming out of it: and wee had founding then, foure and thirtie fathoms water. Wee all conceiued hope of this Northerly Riuer or Sound, and fayling in it, wee found three and twentie fathomes for three leagues, and after twentie fathomes for fiue or fixe leagues, all tough Ozie ground. Then the winde vered more Northerly, and the ftreame came downe fo ftrong, that wee could doe no good on it: wee came to anchor, and went to fupper, and then prefently I fent my Mate *Inet*, with fiue more of our companie in our Boat, with Sayle and Oares to get vp the Riuer, being prouided with Victuall and Weapons for defence, willing them to found as they went; and if it did continue ftill deepe, to goe vntill it did trende to the Eaftward, or to the Southwards, and wee rode ftill.

The fift, in the morning we had the wind at Weft: we began to weigh anchor, purpofing to fet fayle and to runne vp the Sound after our companie: then the wind vered Northerly vpon vs, and we faued our labour. At noone our companie came aboord vs hauing had a hard rought; for they had beene vp the Riuer fixe or feuen leagues, and founded it from twentie to three and twentie; and after brought it to eight, fixe, and one fathome; and then to foure foot in the beft: they then went afhoare, and found good ftore of wilde Goofe quills, a piece of an old Oare, and fome Flowers, and greene things which they found growing: they faw many Deere, and fo did we in our after-dayes fayling. They being come aboord, we prefently fet fayle with the wind at North North-weft, and we ftood out againe to the South-weftwards, with forrow that our labour was in vaine: for, had this Sound held as it did make fhew of, for breadth, depth, fafeneffe of harbour, and good anchor ground, it might haue yeelded an excellent paffage to a more Eafterly Sea. Generally, all the Land of *Noua Zembla* that yet wee haue feene, is to a mans eye a pleafant Land; much mayne high Land with no Snow on it, looking in fome places greene, and Deere feeding thereon: and the Hills are partly couered with Snow, and partly bare. It is no maruell that there is fo much Ice in the Sea toward the Pole, fo many Sounds and Riuers being in the Lands of *Noua Zembla*, and *Newland* to ingender it; befides the coafts of *Pechora*, *Ruffia*, and *Groenland*, with *Lappia*, as by proofes I finde by my trauell in thefe parts: by meanes of which Ice I fuppofe there will be no nauigable paffage this way. This Eeuening wee had the wind at Weft and by South: wee therefore came to anchor vnder *Deere* Point; and it was a ftorme at Sea, wee rode in twentie fathomes, Ozie ground: I fent my Mate, *Ladlow*, with foure more afhoare to fee whether any Morfes were on the fhoare, and to kill fome Fowle, (for we had feene no Morfes fince Saturday, the fecond day of this moneth, that wee faw them driuing out of the Ice.) They found good landing for them, but no figne that they had beene there: but they found that fire had beene made there, yet not lately. At ten of the clocke in the Eeuening, they came aboord, and brought with them neere an hundred Fowles called Wellocks; this night it was wet fogge, and very thicke and cold, the winde at Weft South-weft.

The fixt, in the morning wee had the wind ftormie and fhifting; betweene the Weft and South-weft, againft vs for doing any good: we rode ftill and had much Ice driuing by vs to the Eaftward of vs. At nine of the clocke, this Eeuening wee had the wind at North North-weft: we prefently weighed, and fet fayle, and ftood to the Weftward, being out of hope to find paffage by the North-eaft: And my purpofe was now to fee whether *Willoughbies* Land were, as it is layd in our Cardes; which if it were, wee might finde Morfes on it; for with the Ice they were all driuen from hence. This place vpon *Noua Zembla*, is another then that which the *Hollanders* call *Cofting Sarch*, difcouered by *Oliuer Brownell*: and *William Barentfons* obferuation doth witneffe the fame. It it layd in plot by the *Hollanders* out of his true place too farre North: to what end I know not, vnleffe to make it hold courfe with the Compaffe, not refpecting the variation. It is as broad and like to yeeld paffage as the *Vaygats*, and my hope was, that by the ftrong ftreame it would haue cleered it felfe; but it did not. It is fo full of Ice that you will hardly thinke it. All this day, for the moft part, it was fogge and cold.

The feuenth, cleere but cold weather: in the morning the wind was at the North; from the laft Eeuening to this morning, we fet faile and kept our courfe Weft and by South, fifteene leagues. from morning to eight a clocke in the Eeuening it was calme: then we had the wind againe at North, and we fayled till nine a clocke next morning Weft South-weft, eight leagues; then the wind being Weft and by South, wee went North and by Weft, three leagues; and wee had the Sunne at the higheft South South-weft, in the latitude of 71. degrees 2. minutes. The eight, faire weather; at noone we had the wind at Eaft North-eaft, we ftood North three leagues till foure a clocke: then the wind being at weft and by North, wee ftemmed North and by Weft one league and a halfe, till fix a clocke in the Eeuening; then the wind was at North-eaft a hard gale, and wee ftood till next day at noone Weft and by North, by account three and twentie leagues: we had the Sunne on the Meridian, South and by Weft, halfe a point neereft Weft, in

Marginal notes:

The Riuer fearched.

Noua Zembla pleafant to the eye.

Caufe of much Ice in thofe Seas, which make no nauigable paffage.

Willoughbies Land, a conceit of Cardmakers: it feeming to be no other then *Newland* or *Greenland* (as is before obferued cap.2.) as *Cofting Sarch* of *Brunell* is to others *Noua Zembla*. Note.

the latitude of 70. degrees 41. minutes. The ninth, cleere weather: from this to the next day at noone, we sayled South-west and by West, twelue leagues, and Northward three leagues: and in these courses had these soundings, 41. 42. 46. 48. and 45. fathoms: we had the Sunne South and by VVest, halfe a point to the VVest part of the Compasse. The Sea was loftie: our latitude was 70. degrees 20. minutes.

The tenth, cleere but close weather: from this till next day noone, wee had little wind at West North-west: by account we made our way fiue leagues North-easterly. Wee had the Sun at the highest on the South and by West point, and a terce Westward, in the latitude of 70. degrees 55. minutes, and I thinke we had a rustling tide vnder vs; and in this time had sounding betweene fortie fiue and fortie fathomes, white sand. The eleuenth, cleere weather: from this to the next day at noone, little wind at North North-east, and sometimes calme; wee sayled West and by North by account fiue leagues; and had the Sunne on the Meridian on the South and by West point ¼. West in the latitude of 70. degrees 26. minutes, and found a rustling vn- **10** der vs. This fore-noone we were come into a greene Sea, of the colour of the mayne Ocean,

Greene Sea.

which we first lost the eight of Iune: since which time wee haue had a Sea of a blacke blue colour, which (both by the last and this yeeres experience) is a Sea pestered with Ice.

The twelfth, faire weather: from noone to mid-night wee had the wind shifting betweene the North and West; our course was betweene VVest North-west, and South South-west. Then we had the wind at South, we sayled till the next day at noone, West and by North, thirteene leagues: wee accounted our way from the last day till this day noone Westward, eigh- **20** teene leagues. This after-noone wee saw more Porpoises then in all our Voyage afore. The thirteenth, close weather: in the after-noone hauing much wind at South, with short sayle we stood away West and by North, till eight a clocke in the Eeuening: then we had the wind at South, but most times calme till noone the next day: wee stood away as afore, foure leagues, which made in all twelue leagues: we had the Sunne ere it began to fall, South and by West, in the latitude of 70. degrees 22. minutes.

The fourteenth, wee stood West North-west till mid-night, seuenteene leagues: then the wind scanted and came at West, we stood North North-west, one league and a halfe; then the wind being more Southerly, wee sayled West North-west, fiue leagues. From the last till this day at noone, our way was out of diuers courses North-west and by West, foure and twentie **30** leagues. We had the Sunne beginning to fall at South and by West, in the latitude of 70. degrees 54. minutes.

Thunder.

The fifteenth, faire; but towards night like to be stormie with thunder, the wind betweene South and South South-east; from this, till the sixteenth day at noone, our course was West and by North, seuen and twentie leagues, and the Sunne then began to fall at South, three quarters of a point Westward, in the latitude of 70. degrees 42. minutes. The sixteenth, faire; our way was from this till next day at noone North-west, twelue leagues, out of diuers courses: and we had the wind shifting, sometimes at East, at West South-west, and West and by North; the latitude by a bad obseruation, 71. degrees 44. minutes. The seuenteenth, in the fore-noone faire; the wind being at West and by North. At foure a clocke this morning we saw Land beare **40** off vs, West and South South-west, which was about *Ward-house*: this after-noone wee had a storme at West and by North, we layed it to trie till eight a clocke in the Eeuening, and then set sayle with the wind betweene West North-west, and North-west: our course till the next day at noone, was South-west and by South, twelue leagues: the Cape *Hopewell* bore off vs South South-west, and we were foure or fiue leagues from land.

The eighteenth, gusty, with raine all the fore-noone; then we had the wind shifting till next day at noone from South South-east to East, and South-east: our course in generall was Northwest, foure and twentie leagues: then did North *Kene* beare off vs West halfe a point Southward, being from vs foure leagues; and the North Cape in sight bearing West and by North, &c.

No night in ten weekes.

The seuen and twentieth, cold with raine and storme; this night we began to burne Candle in the Betacle, which we had not done since the nineteenth of May: by reason wee had alwaies **50** day from thence till now. The thirtieth, we had the Sunne vpon the Meridian due South, in the latitude of 68. degrees 46. minutes; whereby we found vs to bee afore our ship, ten or twelue leagues, and *Lowfoot* bore East of vs, but not in sight.

The seuenth of August, I vsed all diligence to arriue at *London*, and therefore now I gaue my companie a certificate vnder my hand, of my free and willing returne, without perswasion or force of any one or more of them: for at my being at *Noua Zembla*, the sixt of Iuly, voide of hope of a North-east passage, (except by the *Vaygats*, for which I was not fitted to trie or proue) I therefore resolued to vse all meanes I could to sayle to the North-west; considering the time and meanes wee had, if the wind should friend vs, as in the first part of our Voyage it

See Hak.10.3.

had done, and to make triall of that place called *Lumleys Inlet*, and the furious ouer-fall by Cap- **60** tayne *Dauis*, hoping to runne into it an hundred leagues, and to returne as God should enable mee. But now hauing spent more then halfe the time I had, and gone but the shortest part of the way, by meanes of contrary winds; I thought it my dutie to saue Victuall, Wages, and

Tackle

Tackle, by my speedy returne, and not by foolish rashnesse, the time being wasted, to lay more charge vpon the action then necessitie should compell, I arriued at *Grauesend* the six and twentieth of August.

CHAP. XVI.

The third Voyage of Master HENRIE HVDSON *toward* Noua Zembla, *and at his returne, his passing from* Farre Ilands *, to* New-found Land, *and along to fortie foure degrees and ten minutes, and thence to* Cape Cod, *and so to thirtie three degrees; and along the Coast to the Northward, to fortie two degrees and an halfe, and vp the Riuer neere to fortie three degrees. Written by* ROBERT IVET *of* Lime-house.

N Saturday the fiue and twentieth of March, 1609. after the old Account, we set sayle from *Amsterdam*; and by the seuen and twentieth day, we were downe at the *Texel:* and by twelue of the clocke we were off the Land, it being East of vs two leagues off. And because it is a journey vsually knowne, I omit to put downe what passed, till we came to the height of *The North Cape of Finmarke*, which we did performe by the fift of May *(stilo nouo)* being Tuesday. On which day we obserued the height of the Pole, and found it to bee 71. degrees and 46. minutes; and found our Compasse to vary six degrees to the West: and at twelue of the clocke, the North Cape did beare South-west and by South, tenne leagues off, and wee steered away East and by South, and East.

After much trouble with fogges, sometimes, and more dangerous of Ice. The nineteenth, being Tuesday, was close stormie weather, with much wind and snow, and very cold: the wind variable betweene the North North-west, and North-east. We made our way West and by North till noone. Then we obserued the Sunne hauing a slake, and found our heigth to bee 70. degrees 30. minutes. And the ship had out-runne vs twentie leagues, by reason of the set of the streame of *The White Sea:* and we had sight of *Wardhouse.* Then at two of the clocke wee tackt to the Eastward: for we could not get about the North Cape, the wind was so scant; and at eight of the clocke at night, on the one and twentieth, the North Cape did beare South-east and by South seuen leagues off. And at mid-night *Assumption* Point did beare South and by East, fiue leagues off vs.

The two and twentieth, gusting weather with haile and snow, the Sunne breaking out sometimes: we continued our course along the Land West South-west. And at tenne of the clocke at night we were thwart off *Zenam.* The bodie of it did beare East off vs fiue leagues: and the course from the North Cape to *Zenam*, is for the most part West and by South, and West South-west, fiftie foure leagues.

The three and twentieth, faire Sun-shining weather; the wind at East and by South, and East South-east, wee steered along the Land South-west, and South-west and by West, eight leagues a Watch, for so we found the Land to lye from *Zenam* to *Lofoote.* And the distance is fiftie leagues from the bodie of *Zenam*, to the Westermost Land of *Lofoote.* And from the one to the other, the course is South-west and by West. For the Needle of our Compasse was set right to the North. At twelue of the clocke at night, the bodie of *Lofoote* did beare South-east, sixe leagues off.

The foure and twentieth, faire cleere Sun-shining weather: the wind variable vpon all points of the Compasse, but most vpon the South-east, and sometimes calme. We continued our course West South-west as before. And at eight of the clocke at night, the Souther part of *Lofoote* did beare South-east ten leagues off vs.

The fiue and twentieth, much wind at North-east, with some snow and haile. The first watch the wind came to the East a fine gale, and so came to the North-east, the second watch at foure of the clocke, and freshed in: And at eight of the clocke it grew to a storme, and so continued. At noone we obserued, and made the ship to be in 67. degrees 58. minutes. Wee continued our course South-west, twelue leagues a watch. At nine of the clocke, *Lofoote* did beare East off vs 15. leagues off. And we found the Compasse to haue no variation. The wind increased to a storme.

The six and twentieth, was a great storme at the North North-east, and North-east. Wee steered away South-west afore the wind with our fore-course abroad: for wee were able to maintayne no more sayles, it blew so vehemently, and the Sea went so high, and brake withall, that it would haue dangered a small ship to lye vnder the Sea. So we skudded seuenty leagues in foure and twentie houres. The storme began to cease at foure of the clocke.

The seuen and twentieth, indifferent faire weather, but a good stiffe gale of wind at North, and

Side notes:
May 5. stilo nouo.

Beala Mare. Wardhouse. They doubled the North Cape. Assumption Point.

Zenam.

Lofoote.

No variation.

A great current ſetting to the North-eaſt.

and North North-eaſt, wee held on our courſe as before. At noone wee obſerued and found our heigth to be 64. degrees 10. minutes. And wee perceiued, that the Current had hindred vs in fortie eight houres to the number of 16. leagues to our beſt iudgement. We ſet our mayne-ſayle, ſprit-ſayle, and our mayne-top-ſayle, and held on our courſe all night, hauing faire weather.

The eight and twentieth, faire weather and little wind at North-eaſt, we held on our courſe South-weſt. At noone wee obſerued the heigth, and were in 62. degrees and 30. minutes. The after-noone was little wind at North North-weſt. The ſecond watch it fell calme. At foure of the clocke wee had ſight of the Iles called *Farre*, and found them to lye out of their place in the Sea Chart fourteene leagues to farre Weſterly. For in running South-weſt from *Lofoote*, wee had a good care to our ſteerage and obſeruations; and counted our ſelues thirtie leagues off by our courſe and obſeruation : and had ſight of them ſixteene or eighteene leagues off. [10]

Farre Iles ſet 14.leagues to farre Weſt.

The nine and twentieth, faire weather ſometimes calme , and ſometimes a gale with the wind varying at South-weſt, and ſo to the North-eaſt. Wee got to the Ilands, but could not gee in. So we ſtood along the Ilands. The ebbe being come, we durſt not put in.

Stromo.

The thirtieth faire weather ; the wind at South.eaſt and Eaſt South-eaſt. In the morning we turned into a Road in *Stromo*, one of the Ilands of *Farre*, betweene *Stromo* and *Mugge-nes*,and got in by nine of the clocke : for it flowed ſo there that day. And aſſoone as we came in, we went to Romage ,and ſent our Boat for water, and filled all our emptie Caskes with freſh water. Wee made an end of our Romaging this night by ten of the clocke.

The one and thirtieth, faire Sun-ſhining weather, the wind at Eaſt South-eaſt. In the fore-[20] noone our Maſter with moſt of his Company went on ſhoare to walke, and at one of the clocke they returned aboord. Then we ſet ſayle.

Iune.

The firſt of Iune, *ſtilo nouo*, faire Sun-ſhining weather, the wind at Eaſt South-eaſt. We continued on our courſe South-weſt and by Weſt. At noone wee obſerued the Sunne, and found our heigth to be 60. degrees 58. minutes : and ſo continued on our courſe all night with faire weather. This night we lighted Candles in the m Bittacle againe.

m The Bittacle is a cloſe place in which the Compaſſe ſtandeth. Buſſe Iland. Their firſt ſight of ſtars: for further North, they had continuall Sun-light. Change of water.

The ſecond myſtie weather, the wind at North-eaſt. At noone we ſteered away Weſt South-weſt, to find *Buſſe* Iland, diſcouered in the yeere 1578. by one of the ſhips of Sir *Martin Frobiſher*, to ſee if it lay in her true latitude in the Chart or no : wee continued our courſe as before all night, with a faire gale of wind : this night we had ſight of the firſt ſtars, and our water was [30] changed colour to a white greene. The Compaſſe had no variation.

A ſtrange current out of the South-weſt.

The third, faire Sun-ſhining weather;the wind at North-eaſt. We ſteered on our courſe South-weſt and by Weſt, with a ſtiffe gale of wind. At noone we obſerued and found our heigth to bee 58. degrees 48. minutes. And I was before the ſhip 16. leagues , by reaſon of the Current that held vs ſo ſtrong out of the South-weſt. For it is eight leagues in foure and twentie houres.We accounted our ſelues neere *Buſſe* Iland : by mid-night we looked out for it,but could not ſee it.

The fourth, in the morning was much wind with fogge and raine. Wee ſteered away South-weſt by weſt all the fore-noone, the wind ſo increaſing , that wee were enforced to take in our top-ſayle : the winde continuing ſo all the after-noone. Wee ſteered away South-weſt all the fore-part of the night;and at ten of the clocke at night it was little wind;and that was at South, [40] and ſo came vp to the South South-eaſt.

The fiſt, ſtormie weather, and much wind at South , and South by Eaſt, ſo that at foure of the clocke in the morning, we tooke in our fore-ſayle, and lay a try with our mayne corſe, and tryed away Weſt North-weſt foure leagues. But at noone it was leſſe wind , and the Sunne ſhewed forth; and we obſerued, and found our heigth to be 56.degrees 21.minutes. In the after-noone the wind vered to and fro betweene the South-weſt and the South-eaſt , with raine and fogge, and ſo continued all night. Wee found that our ſhip had gone to the Weſtward of our courſe. The ſixth, thicke haſie weather with guſts of wind, and ſhowers of raine. The wind varied betweene Eaſt South-Eaſt and South-weſt , wee ſteered on many courſes a Weſt South-weſt way. The afternoone watch the wind was at Eaſt South-eaſt, a ſtiffe gale with myſt and [50] raine. Wee ſteered away South-weſt, by Weſt eight leagues. At noone the Sunne ſhone forth, and we found the heigth to bee 56. degrees 8. minutes. The ſeuenth, faire ſun-ſhining weather all the fore-noone, and calme vntill twelue of the clocke. In the after-noone the wind came to the North-weſt,a ſtiffe gale. We ſteered South-weſt by Weſt, and made a South-weſt way. At noone we fonnd the height to bee 55. degrees one minute, and it continued all night a hard gale.

Note well.

Bonets are thoſe which are liced and ecked to the ſayles to enlarge them : with reference whereto the mayne courſe, miſſen courſe, fore courſe,is vnderſtood of thoſe ſayles without their Bonets.

The eight, ſtormy weather, the wind variable, betweene Weſt and North-weſt much wind : at eight of the clocke wee tooke off our Bonnets. At noone the Sunne ſhewed forth, and wee obſerued,and our height was 54.degree, 30.minutes. The ninth,faire ſun-ſhining weather,and little wind all the fore-part of the day vntill eleuen of the clocke. Then the wind came to the South South-eaſt,and we ſteered away Weſt South-weſt. At noone we found our height to bee [60] 53. degrees and 45.minutes,and we had made our way South by Weſt ten leagues. In the afternoone the wind increaſed and continued all night at Eaſt North-eaſt and Eaſt.

The twelfth,faire weather, the wind variable betweene Eaſt North-eaſt and South-eaſt, wee ſteered on our courſe as before.At foure of the clock in the afternoon the wind came vp at South-

eaſt.

east. And we held our course as before. At noone wee obserued and found our height to be 52. degrees 35. minutes.

The eleuenth, in the morning was thicke and foggie, the winde varying betweeene South South-west, and North-west. At foure of the clocke in the morning, wee tackt about to the Southward: At eleuen of the clocke the winde came to the North-west, and so to the West North-west. This day we had change of water, of a whitish greene, like to the Ice water to the North-west. At noone it cleered vp, and became very faire weather: wee put out our mayne top-sayle: then we obserued the Sunne, and found our height to be 51. degrees 24. minutes. We had sayled many courses and found our ship gone to the Southward of our account ten leagues, by reason of a current from the North-ward. The Compasse varied on point to the East.

A current from the North. Variation one point East.

The twelfth, faire Sun-shining weather, but much wind at the West: we stood to the Southward all day, the wind shifting betweene the South-west and the West and by North. Wee made our way South halfe a point West, eight and twentie leagues. Our height at noone was 50. degrees 9. minutes. At eight of the clock at night we took off our Bonets, the wind increasing.

The thirteenth, faire Sun-shining weather: the wind variable betweene the West, and North North-west. We made our way South South-west seuen and twentie leagues. At noone we obserued, and found our heigth to be 48. degrees 45. minutes. But not to be trusted, the Sea went so high. In the after-noone the winde was calmer, and wee brought to our Bonets, and stood to the Southward all night with a stiffe gale.

The fourteenth, faire and cleere Sun-shining weather: the winde variable betweene the North-west and South-west by West. At mid-night I obserued the North starre at a North-west by West Guarde; a good obseruation 49. degrees 30. minutes. And at noone wee obserued the Sunne, and our heigth was 48. degrees 6. minutes. And I made account we ranne betweene the two obseruations twelue leagues. At one of the clocke in the after-noone, wee cast about to the Westward, and stood so all night: the winde increased to a storme, and was very much winde with Raine.

Latitutde 48. degrees 6. minutes.

The fifteenth, we had a great storme, and spent * ouer-boord our fore-mast, bearing our fore corse low set. The sixteenth, we were forced to trie with our mayne sayle, by reason of the vnconstant weather. So wee tried foure watches South-east and by South eight leagues and an halfe, and two watches sixe leagues. The seuenteenth, reasonable faire weather: the wind variable betweene West South-west, and West North-west. And a stiffe gale of wind, and so great a swelling Sea out of the West South-west, that wee could doe nothing. So one watch and an halfe wee droue North foure leagues and an halfe, and foure watches and an halfe South and by East halfe a point East twelue leagues. The eighteenth, reasonable weather but close and cloudie, and an hard gale of wind, and a great Sea. The winde being at the North-west, wee lay to the Southward, and made our drift South and by West, fiue leagues. The after-noone prooued little wind, and the night part calme. The nineteenth, in the fore-noone faire weather and calme. In the morning we set the piece of our fore mast, and set our fore corse.

* To spend the Mast, is vnderstood of breaking it by foule weather only.

The one and twentieth, faire Sun-shining weather, but much wind and a great Sea. We split our fore saile at ten of the clocke; then we laid it a trie * with our mayne sayle, and continued so all day. In the night it fell to be little wind. This day our heigth was 45. degrees 48. minutes.

* That is, bare no more sayle but the mayne sayle, &c. Variation.

The two and twentieth, very faire Sun-shining weather, and calme all the after-noone. At noone we made a very good obseruation, and found our heigth 44. degrees 58. minutes. At eight of the clocke at night wee had a small gale of winde at South-east. And wee steered away West for *Newfonnd* Land. The true Compasse varied one point East.

The three and twentieth, thicke weather with much wind and some raine. At eight of the clocke in the morning, the wind came to the West South-west, and West so stiffe a gale, that we were forced to take our top-sayle, and steered away North North-west vntill foure of the clock in the after-noone. Then we tact to the Southward the winde at West North-west. At eight of the clocke at night wee tooke in our top-sayles, and laid it a trie with our mayne sayle, the winde at West.

The foure and twentieth, a stiffe gale of wind, varying betweene the West and North North-west, we tried till sixe of the clocke: at which time we set our foresaile, and steered way West and by South by our Compasse eight leagues in foure watches: and wee tried away South in one watch and an halfe.

The fiue and twentieth, faire Sun-shining weather, the wind at North North-west and North, we steered away West by South by our Compasse till twelue of the clocke: at which time we had sight of a sayle, and gaue her chase but could not speake with her. She stood to the Eastward; and we stood after her till sixe of the clocke in the after-noone. Then wee tact to the Westward againe, and stood on our course. It was faire all night, and little wind sometimes.

The six and twentieth, all the fore-part of the day very faire weather and hot, but at foure of the clocke in the after-noone it grew to bee much winde and raine: the winde was at South South-east. At noone wee obserued and found our heigth to bee 44. degrees 33. minutes. At eight of the clocke at night, the wind came to South-west, and West South-west, Wee steered

North-

North-west, one Watch, and at twelue in the night, to the West, and West and by South, very much wind. So we could lye but North North-west.

The seuen and twentieth, very much winde and a soare storme, the wind Westerly. In the morning at foure of the clocke, wee tooke in our fore-corse, and layd it a trie with our mayne-corse low set; and so continued all the day and night, two watches to the Northward. At eight of the clocke at night, we tackt to the Southward.

The eight and twentieth, faire sun-shining weather, the wind at West and by South; we lay a trie to the Southward till eight of the clocke in the morning. Then wee set our fore-corse, and stood to the Southward a stiffe gale of wind, but faire weather and a great Sea, out of the Wester-boord, and so continued all night.

10

The nine and twentieth, faire sun-shining weather, the wind at West and by South; we stood to the Southward vntill sixe of the clocke at night, and made our way South and by East, foure leagues. Then the winde came to the South-west, and wee cast about to the VVestward, and made our way VVest North-west all night. At noone, I found the height 43. degrees 6. minutes. The variation one point VVest.

The thirtieth, faire sun-shining weather, the winde at South-west and by VVest, we steered North-west and by VVest. And made our way so, by reason of the variation of the Compasse. At noone, I found the height to bee 43. degrees 18. minutes; wee continued our course all night, and made our way North-west and by VVest, halfe a point VVesterly, fiue and twentie leagues.

Iuly.   The first of Iuly, close, mystie and thicke weather, but a faire gale of wind at South-west, and 20 South-west by South. We steered away North-west and by West, Westerly, and made our way so, by reason of the variation of the Compasse. At eight of the clocke at night, wee sounded for the Banke of *New-found Land*, but could get no ground.

The Banke of   The second, thicke mystie weather, but little wind, and that at West, and West and by South.
New found Land At eight of the clocke in the morning, we cast about to the Southward, and when our ship was on stayes, we sounded for the Banke, and had ground in thirtie fathoms, white sand and shells, and presently it cleered: and we had sight of a sayle, but spake not with her. In the night we had much Rayne, Thunder and Lightning, and wind shifting.

Variation west   The third, faire Sun-shining weather, with a faire gale of wind at East North-east, and wee
17. degrees.   steered away West South-west by our Compasse, which varyed 17. degrees Westward. This 30
French-men Fi-   morning we were among a great Fleet of *French*-men, which lay Fishing on the Banke; but we
shing on the   spake with none of them. At noone wee found our heighth to bee 43. degrees 41. minutes. And
Banke.   we sounded at ten of the clocke, and had thirtie fathoms gray sand. At two of the clocke wee sounded, and had fiue and thirtie fathoms gray sand. At eight of the clocke at night, we sounded againe, and had eight and thirtie fathoms gray sand, as before.

The fourth, at the fore-part of the day cleere, with a faire gale of wind, but variable betweene the East North-east, and South and by East, wee held on our course as before. The after-noone was mystie, the wind shifting betweene the South and the West, till foure of the clocke. Then we tooke in our top-sayle and sprit-sayle, and sounded and had no ground in seuentie fathoms. The winde shifted still vntill eight of the clocke, then it came to the North North-east, and 40
Variation 15.   North-east and by North, and we steered away West North-west, by our varyed Compasse,
degrees North-   which made a West way halfe point North. The Compasse varyed 15. degrees from the North
west.   to the West.

The fift, faire sun-shining weather, the wind at North-east and by North, we steered away West North-west, which was West halfe a point North. At noone we found our heighth to be 44. degrees 10. minutes, and sounded, and had no ground in one hundred fathoms. The after-noone proued calme sometimes, and somtimes little wind, vntill nine of the clocke in the night. Then the wind came to the East, and we held on our course. At mid-night I obserued and found
Variation 13.   the height to bee 44. degrees 10. minutes, by the North Starre and the *Scorpions* heart. The
degrees.   Compasse varyed 13. degrees.

50

The sixth, the fore-part of the day faire weather, and a stiffe gale of wind, betweene South South-east, and South-west, wee steered West and by North, and West North-west. The after-part of the day from two of the clocke, was all foggie and thicke weather; the wind a hard gale,
Foggie and   varying betweene South-west and by South, and West and by North, we made our way North-
thick weather.   west halfe a point Northerly, nineteene leagues, vpon many points foure Watches. At night at eight of the clocke, we sounded and had no ground at one hundred fathoms.

The seuenth, faire sun-shining weather, the wind varying betweene West and by North, and West and by South. At foure of the clocke in the morning, we cast about to the Southward, and stood so till one in the after-noone. At noone we found our height to be 44. degrees 26. minutes. At seuen of the clocke, we tackt to the Northward. At eight at night, we tackt to the South- 60
ward, and sounded, and had nine and fiftie fathoms, white sand.

The eight, in the fore-noone faire weather, but the morning foggie till seuen of the clocke. At foure of the clocke in the morning we sounded, and had fiue & fortie fathoms, fine white sand, and we had runne fiue leagues South and by West. Then wee stood along one Glasse, and went

one

one league as before. Then we ftood one Glaffe and founded, and had fixtie fathoms. Then wee takt and ftood backe to the Banke, and had fiue and twentie fathoms ; and tryed for Fifh, and it tell calme, and we caught one hundred and eighteene great Coddes, from eight a clocke till one, and after Dinner wee tooke twelue, and faw many great Scoales of Herrings. Then wee had a gale of wind at South, and it fhifted to the Weft North-weft , and we ftood three Glaffes and founded and had fixtie fathomes, and ftood two Glaffes, and had two and fortie fathoms, red ftones and fhells. So wee founded euery Glaffe and had feuerall foundings 35. 33. 30. 31. 32. 33. and 34. fathoms.

Many great Cods taken. Many great Scoales of Herrings. To found is to trie the depth by Line and Lead, or Pole, &c.

10 The ninth, faire calme weather, we lay becalmed all day and caught fome Fifh, but not much, becaufe we had fmall ftore of falt. At three of the clocke in the after-noone, wee had a gale at South-eaft, and South South-eaft, and we fteered away Wefterly, our Compaffe was Weft and by South halfe a point South. At foure of the clocke, we founded and had but fifteene, feuenteene, and nineteene fathoms on a fifhing Banke ; and we founded euery Glaffe. Then we could get no ground in fiue and twentie fathoms, and had fight of a fayle on head off vs. At noone our height was 44. degrees 27. minutes. We ftood to the Weftward all night, and fpake with a *French*-man, which lay Fifhing on the Banke of *Sablen*, in thirtie fathoms, and we faw two or three more.

The tenth, very myftie and thicke weather, the wind at South-weft, a faire gale. We ftood to the South-ward, and made our way South-eaft and by Eaft. At twelue of the clocke we founded, and had eight and fortie fathoms : againe at two we founded, and had fiftie fathoms. And 20 at fixe of the clocke we founded : and had eight and fortie fathoms on the end of the Banke. Againe, at eight of the clocke at night wee founded, and had no ground in eightie fathomes, and were ouer the Banke. So wee ftood along till mid-night. The Compaffe varyed 17. degrees to the Weftward.

Variation 17. degrees.

The eleuenth, very thicke and myftie weather. At twelue of the clocke at night, we caft about to the Weftward, and ftood fo all day, and made our way Weft North-weft. We founded at twelue of the clocke, but had no ground ; fo we ftood to the Weftward all the fore-part of the night, and founded but could get no ground in fiftie or fixtie fathoms till mid-night. Then I founded and had ground at fifteene fathoms, white fand.

The twelfth, was very foggie, we ftood our courfe all the morning till eleuen of the clocke ; at 30 which time we had fight of the Land, which is low white fandie ground, right on head off vs ; and had ten fathoms. Then we tackt to the Southward, and ftood off foure Glaffes : then we tackt to the Land againe, thinking to haue rode vnder it, and as we came neere it, the fog was fo thicke that we could not fee ; fo wee ftood off againe. From mid-night to two of the clocke, we came founding in twelue, thirteene, and foureteene fathoms off the fhoare. At foure of the clocke, we had 20 fathoms. At eight of the clocke at night 30. fathoms. At twelue of the clocke 65. fathoms, and but little winde, for it deeped apace, but the neerer the fhoare the fairer fhoalding.

Land, being low, white and fandie.

The thirteenth, faire fun-fhining weather, from eight of the clocke in the fore-noone all day after, but in the morning it was foggie. Then at eight of the clocke we caft about for the fhoare, but could not fee it ; the wind being at South by our true Compaffe, wee fteered VVeft and by 40 North. At noone we obferued, and found our height to bee 43. degrees 25. minutes ; fo we fteered away VVeft and by North all the after-noone. At foure of the clocke in the after-noone, we founded and had fiue and thirtie fathoms. And at fixe of the clocke, wee had fight of the Land, and faw two fayles on head off vs. The land by the waters fide is low Land, and white fandie Bankes rifing full of little Hils. Our foundings were 35. 33. 30. 28. 32. 37. 33. & 32. fathoms.

43. degrees 25. minutes. Sight of Land againe, and of two Ships.

The foureteenth, full of myfts flying and vading, the wind betweene South and South-weft, we fteered away Weft North-weft, and North-weft and by Weft. Our foundings were 29. 25. 24. 25. 22. 25. 27. 30. 28. 30. 35. 43. 50. 70. 90. 70. 64. 86. 100. fathoms, and no ground.

The fifteenth, very myftie, the winde varying betweene South and South-weft, wee fteered Weft and by North, and VVeft North-weft. In the morning we founded, and had one hundred fathoms, till foure of the clocke in the after-noone. Then we founded againe, and had feuentie 50 fiue fathoms. Then in two Glaffes running, which was not aboue two *English* miles, we founded and had fixtie fathoms, and it fhoalded a great pace vntill we came to twentie fathoms. Then we made account we were neere the Ilands that lie off the fhoare. So we came to an Anchor, the Sea being very fmooth and little wind, at nine of the clocke at night. After fupper, we tryed for Fifh, and I caught fifteene Cods, fome the greateft that I haue feene, and fo we rode all night.

The fixteenth, in the morning it cleered vp, and wee had fight of fiue Ilands lying North, and North and by VVeft from vs, two leagues. Then wee made ready to fet fayle, but the myft came fo thicke, that we durft not enter in among them.

Fiue Ilands.

The feuenteenth, was all myftie, fo that wee could not get into the Harbour. At ten of the 60 clocke two Boates came off to vs, with fixe of the *Sauages* of the Countrey, feeming glad of our comming. VVe gaue them trifles, and they eate and dranke with vs ; and told vs, that there were Gold, Siluer, and Copper mynes hard by vs ; and that the *French*-men doe Trade with them ; which is very likely, for one of them fpake fome words of *French*. So wee rode ftill all day and all night, the weather continuing myftie.

Sixe *Sauages* come aboord them.

The

A large Riuer.
The eighteenth, faire weather, wee went into a very good Harbour, and rode hard by the ſhoare in foure fathoms water. The Riuer runneth vp a great way, but there is but two fathoms 44.Degrees 10. minutes. hard by vs. VVe went on ſhoare and cut vs a fore Maſt, then at noone we came aboord againe, and found the height of the place to bee in 44. degrees 1. minute ; and the Sunne to fall at a South South-weſt Sunne. VVe mended our ſayles,and fell to make our fore-Maſt. The Harbour lyeth South and North, a mile in where we rode.

The nineteenth, we had faire ſun-ſhining weather, we rode ſtill. In the after-noone wee went with our Boate to looke for freſh water, and found ſome ; and found a ſhoald with many Lobſters on it,and caught one and thirtie. The people comming aboord,ſhewed vs great friend-ſhip, but we could not truſt them. The twentieth, faire ſunne-ſhining weather, the winde at South-weſt. In the morning,our Scute went out to catch freſh Fiſh halfe an houre before day, ₁₀ and returned in two houres, bringing ſeuen and twentie great Coddes, with two hookes and lines. In the after-noone wee went for more Lobſters, and caught fortie, and returned aboord. Then wee eſpied two *French* Shallops full of the Countrey people come into the Harbour, but The trade of the *French* with the *Saluages*. they offered vs no wrong, ſeeing we ſtood vpon our guard. They brought many Beauer ſkinnes, and other fine Furres, which they would haue changed for redde Gownes. For the *French* trade with them for red Caſſockes, Kniues, Hatchets, Copper, Kettles, Treuits, Beades, and other trifles.

The one and twentieth, all myſtie, the wind Eaſterly, wee rode ſtill and did nothing, but a-bout our Maſt. The two and twentieth, faire Sun-ſhining weather, the winde all Northerly, ₂₀ we rode ſtill all the day. In the after-noone our Scute went to catch more Lobſters,and brought with them nine and fiftie. The night was cleere weather.

The three and twentieth, faire ſun-ſhining weather and very hot. At eleuen of the clocke,our fore Maſt was finiſhed, and we brought it aboord, and ſet it into the ſtep, and in the after-noone we rigged it. This night we had ſome little myſt and rayne.

The foure and twentieth, very hot weather,the winde at South out of the ſea. The fore-part of the day wee brought to our ſayles. In the morning, our Scute went to take Fiſh, and in two houres they brought with them twentie great Coddes, and a great Holibut, the night was faire alſo. We kept good watch for feare of being betrayed by the people, and perceiued where they layd their Shallops.

They ſpoyle Houſes of the *Saluages*.
The fiue and twentieth, very faire weather and hot. In the morning wee manned our Scute ₃₀ with foure Muskets,and ſixe men, and tooke one of their Shallops and brought it aboord. Then we manned our Boat & Scute with twelue men and Muskets,and two ſtone Pieces orMurderers, and draue the *Saluages* from their Houſes, and tooke the ſpoyle of them, as they would haue done of vs. Then wee ſet ſayle, and came downe to the Harbours mouth, and rode there all night, becauſe the winde blew right in, and the night grew myſtie with much rayne till mid-night. Then it fell calme, and the wind came off the Land at Weſt North-weſt, and it began to cleere. The Compaſſe varyed 10. degrees North-weſt.

The ſixe and twentieth, faire and cleere ſunne-ſhining weather. At fiue of the clocke in the morning, the winde being off the ſhoare at North North-weſt,we ſet ſayle and came to ſea, and ₄₀ by noone we counted our ſhip had gone foureteene leagues South-weſt. In the after-noone, the winde ſhifted variably betweene Weſt South-weſt, and North-weſt. At noone, I found the Variation 10. degrees toward the North-weſt height to bee 43 .degrees 56.minutes. This Eeuening being very faire weather, wee obſerued the variation of our Compaſſe at the Sunnes going downe, and found it to bee 10. degrees from the North to the VVeſtward.

The ſeuen and twentieth, faire ſun-ſhining weather, the winde ſhifting betweene the South-weſt,and Weſt and by North,a ſtiffe gale, we ſtood to the Southward all day, and made our way South and by Weſt, ſeuen and twentie leagues. At noone,our height was 42.degrees 50.minuts. At foure of the clocke in the after-noone, wee caſt about to the Northward. At eight of the clocke, we tooke in our top-ſayles and our fore-bonnet, and went with a ſhort ſayle all night. ₅₀

The eight and twentieth, very thicke and myſtie, and a ſtiffe gale of wind, varying betweene South South-weſt,and South-weſt and by VVeſt ; we made our way North-weſt and by VVeſt, ſeuen and twentie leagues, wee ſounded many times and could get no ground. At fiue of the clocke, we caſt about to the Southward, the wind at South-weſt and by VVeſt. At which time Variation 6. degrees to the Weſt. we ſounded, and had ground at ſeuentie fiue fathoms. At eight, wee had ſixtie fiue fathoms. At ten, ſixtie. At twelue of the clocke at mid-night, fiftie ſixe fathoms, gray ſand. The Compaſſe varyed 6. degrees the North point to the VVeſt.

The nine and twentieth,faire weather, we ſtood to the Southward,and made our way South and by VVeſt a point South, eighteene leagues. At noone, we found our height to bee 42. de-grees 56.minutes, wee ſounded oft,and had theſe 60. 64. 65. 67. 65. 65. 70.and 75. fathoms. At ₆₀ Variation 5. & a halfe degrees. night, wee tryed the variation of our Compaſſe by the ſetting of the Sunne, and found that it went downe 37. degrees to the North-ward of the VVeſt, and ſhould haue gone downe but 31. degrees. The Compaſſe varyed 5.½. degrees.

The thirtieth, very hot, all the fore-part of the day calme,the wind at South South-eaſt, wee
ſteered

steered away VVest South-west and founded many times, and could find no ground at one hundred and seuentie fathomes. VVe found a great current and many ouer-falls. Our current had deceiued vs. For at noone we found our height to be 41. degrees 34. minutes. And the current had heaued vs to the Southward fourteene leagues. At eight of the clocke at night, I sounded and had ground in fiftie two fathomes. In the end of the mid-night watch, wee had fiftie three fathomes. This last obseruation is not to be trusted.

A great current and many ouer-fals.

The one and thirtieth, very thicke and mystie all day, vntill tenne of the clocke. At night the wind came to the South, and South-west and South. We made our way West North-west nineteene leagues. Wee sounded many times, and had difference of soundings, sometimes little stones, and sometimes grosse gray sand, fiftie six, fiftie foure, fortie eight, fortie seuen, fortie foure, fortie six, fiftie fathomes; and at eight of the clocke at night it fell calme, and we had fiftie fathomes. And at ten of the clocke we heard a great Rut, like the Rut of the shoare. Then I sounded and found the former Depths; and mistrusting a current, seeing it so still that the ship made no way, I let the lead lie on the ground, and found a tide set to the South-west, and South-west by West, so fast, that I could hardly vere the Line so fast; and presently came an hurling current, or tyde with ouer-fals, which cast our ship round; and the Lead was so fast in the ground, that I feared the Lines breaking, and we had no more but that. At mid-night I sounded againe, and we had seuentie fiue fathomes; and the strong streame had left vs.

A great Rut.

A current to the South-west and South-west by West, with ouer-fals. August.

The first of August, all the fore-part of the day was mystie, and at noone it cleered vp. We found that our height was 41. degrees 45. minutes, and we had gone nineteene leagues. The afternoone was reasonable cleere. We found a rustling tide or current, with many ouer-fals to continue still, and our water to change colour, and our sea to bee very deepe, for wee found no ground in one hundred fathomes. The night was cleere, and the winde came to the North, and North North-east, we steered West.

The second, very faire weather and hot: from the morning till noone we had a gale of wind, but in the after-noone little wind. At noone I sounded and had one hundred and ten fathomes; and our height was 41. degrees 56. minutes. And wee had runne foure and twentie leagues and an halfe. At the Sun-setting we obserued the variation of the Compasse, and found that it was come to his true place. At eight of the clocke the gale increased, so wee ranne sixe leagues that watch, and had a very faire and cleere night.

The third, very hot weather. In the morning, we had sight of the Land, and steered in with it, thinking to goe to the North-ward of it. So we sent our shallop with fiue men, to found in by the shore: and they found it deepe fiue fathomes within a Bow-shot of the shoare; and they went on Land, and found goodly Grapes, and Rose trees, and brought them aboord with them, at fiue of the clocke in the Eeuening. We had seuen and twentie fathomes within two miles of the shoare; and we found a floud come from the South-east, and an ebbe from the North-west, with a very strong streame, and a great hurling and noyses. At eight of the clocke at night, the wind began to blow a fresh gale, and continued all night but variable. Our sounding that wee had to the Land, was one hundred, eightie, seuentie foure, fiftie two, fortie sixe, twentie nine, twentie seuen, twentie foure, nineteene, seuenteene, sometimes Oze, and sometimes gray sand.

They goe on Land neere Cape Cod.

The fourth, was very hot: we stood to the North-west two watches, and one South in for the Land, and came to an Anchor at the Norther end of the Headland, and heard the voyce of men call. Then we sent our Boat on shoare, thinking they had beene some *Christians* left on the Land: but wee found them to bee Sauages, which seemed very glad of our comming. So wee brought one aboord with vs, and gaue him meate, and he did eate and drinke with vs. Our Master gaue him three or foure glasse Buttons, and sent him on Land with our shallop againe. And at our Boats comming from the shoare he leapt and danced, and held vp his hands, and pointed vs to a riuer on the other side: for we had made signes that we came to fish there. The bodie of this Headland lyeth in 41. degrees 45. minutes. We set sayle againe after dinner, thinking to haue got to the Westward of this Headland, but could not; so we beare vp to the Southward of it, & made a South-east way; and the Souther point did beare West at eight of the clocke at night. Our soundings about the Easter and Norther part of this Headland, a league from the shoare are these: at the Easterside thirtie, twentie seuen, twentie seuen, twentie foure, twentie fiue, twentie. The North-east point 17. degrees 18. minutes, and so deeper. The North-end of this Headland, hard by the shoare thirtie fathomes: and three leagues off North North-west, one hundred fathomes. At the South-east part a league off, fifteene, sixteene, and seuenteene fathomes. The people haue greene Tabacco, and pipes, the boles whereof are made of Earth, and the pipes of red Copper. The Land is very sweet.

Sauages.

The fift, all mystie. At eight of the clocke in the morning, wee tackt about to the Westward, and stood in till foure of the clocke in the after-noone; at which time it cleered, and wee had sight of the Head-land againe fiue leagues from vs. The Souther point of it did beare West off vs: and we sounded many times, and had no ground. And at foure of the clocke we cast about, and at our staying wee had seuentie fathomes. Wee steered away South and South by East all night,

night, and could get no ground at seuentie and eightie fathomes. For wee feared a great Riffe, that lyeth off the Land, and steered away South and by East.

The sixth, faire weather, but many times mysting. Wee steered away South South-east, till eight of the clocke in the morning; Then it cleered a little, and wee cast about to the Westward. Then we sounded and had thirtie fathomes, grosse sand, and were come to the Riffe. Then wee kept our Lead, and had quicke shoalding, from thirtie, twentie nine, twentie seuen, twentie foure, twentie two, twentie and an halfe, twentie, twentie, nineteene, nineteene, nineteene, eighteene, eighteene, seuenteene; and so deeping againe as proportionally as it shoalded. For we steered South and South-east till we came to twentie sixe fathomes. Then we steered South-west for so the tyde doth set. By and by it being calme we tryed by our Lead; for you shall 10 haue sixteene or seuenteene fathomes, and the next cast but seuen or six fathomes. And farther to the Westward you shall haue foure and fiue foot water, and see Rockes vnder you; and you shall see the Land in the top. Vpon this Riffe we had an obseruation, and found that it lyeth in 40.

This dangerous Riffe is in 41. degrees 10 minutes, and lyeth off East from Cape Cod into the Sea.

degrees 10. minutes. And this is that Headland which Captaine *Bartholomew Gosnold* discouered in the yeere 1602. and called Cape *Cod*; becauſe of the store of Cod-fish that hee found thereabout. So we steered South-west three leagues, and had twentie, and twentie foure fathomes. Then we steered West two Glasses halfe a league, and came to fifteene fathomes. Then we steered off South-east foure Glasses, but could not get deepe water; for there the tyde of ebbe laid vs on; and the streame did hurle so, that it laid vs so neere the breach of a shoald, that wee were forced to Anchor. So at seuen of the clocke at night, wee were at an Anchor in tenne fathomes: 20 And, I giue God most heartie thankes, the least water wee had was seuen fathomes and an halfe. We rode still all night, and at a still water I sounded so farre round about our ship as we could see a light; and had no lesse then eight, nine, ten, and eleuen fathomes : The myst continued being very thicke.

The seuenth, faire weather and hot, but mystie. Wee rode still hoping it would cleere, but on the floud it fell calme and thicke. So we rode still all day and all night. The floud commeth from the South-west, and riseth not aboue one fathome and an halfe in nepe streames. Toward night it cleered, and I went with our shallop and sounded, and found no lesse water then eight fathomes to the South-east off vs : but we saw to the North-west off vs great Breaches.

The Flats.

The eight, faire and cleere weather. In the morning, by sixe of the clocke at slake water wee 30 weighed; the wind at North-east, and set our fore-sayle and mayne top-sayle, and got a mile o-uer the Flats. Then the tyde of ebbe came, so we anchored againe till the floud came. Then wee set sayle againe, and by the great mercie of God, wee got cleere off them by one of the clocke this after-noone. And wee had sight of the Land from the West North-west, to the North North-west. So we steered away South South-east all night; and had ground vntill the middle of the third watch. Then we had fortie fiue fathomes, white sand, and little stones. So all our soundings are twentie, twentie, twentie two, twentie seuen, thirtie two, fortie three, fortie three, fortie fiue. Then no ground in seuentie fathomes.

The ninth, very faire and hot weather, the wind a very stiffe gale. In the morning, at foure of the clocke, our shallop came running vp against our sterne, and split in all her stemme ; So we 40 were faine to cut her away. Then wee tooke in our mayne sayle, and lay atrie vnder our fore-sayle vntill twelue of the clocke at mid-day. Then the wind ceased to a faire gale, so wee stood away South-west. Then we lay close by, on many courses a South by West way fifteene leagues; and three watches South-east by East, ten leagues. At eight of the clocke at night, wee tooke in our top-sayles, and went with a low sayle ; becauſe we were in an vnknowne sea. At noone we obserued and found our heigth to be 38. degrees 39. minutes.

The tenth, in the morning some raine and cloudie weather : the winde at South-west, wee made our way South-east by East, ten leagues. At noone, wee obserued and found our heigth to bee 38. degrees 39. minutes. Then wee tackt about to the Westward, the wind being at South and by East, little wind. At foure of the clocke it fell calme, and we had two Dolphines about 50 our ship, and many small fishes. At eight of the clocke at night, wee had a small lingring gale. All night we had a great Sea out of the South-west, and another great Sea out of the North-east.

The eleuenth, all the fore-part of the day faire weather, and very hot. Wee stood to the West South-west till noone. Then the wind shorted, and we could lye but South-west and by South. At noone, wee found our heigth to bee 39. degrees 11. minutes. And that the current

A current set-ting to the North. Variation one point.

had laid vs to the Northward thirtie two minutes contrary to our expectation. At foure of the clocke in the after-noone there came a myst, which endured two houres. But wee had it faire and cleere all night after. The Compasse varied the North point to the West one whole point.

The twelfth, faire weather, the wind variable betweene the South-west and by South, and the North little wind. In the morning we killed an extraordinary fish, and stood to the West- 60 ward all day and all night. At noone our found our heigth to be 38. degrees 13. minutes. And

Variation 10. degrees.

the obseruation the day before was not good. This noone, we found the Compasse to vary from the North to the West ten degrees.

The thirteenth, faire weather and hot : the wind at North-east. Wee steered away West and

by

by our Compasse two and twentie leagues. At noone wee found our height to bee 37. degrees 45. minutes, and that our way from noone to noone was West South-west, halfe a point Southerly. The Compasse was 7. degrees and a halfe variation, from the North point to the West.

The fourteenth, faire weather, but cloudie, and a stiffe gale of wind, variable betweene North-east and South-west, wee steered away West by South, a point South all day vntill nine of the clocke at night; then it began to Thunder and Lighten, whereupon we tooke in all our sayles, and layd it a hull, and hulled away North till mid-night, a league and a halfe.

The fifteenth, very faire and hot weather, the winde at North by East. At foure of the clocke in the morning we set sayle, and stood on our course to the Westward. At noone wee found our height to bee 37. degrees 25. minutes. The after-noone proued little wind. At eight of the clocke at night, the winde came to the North, and wee steered West by North, and West North-west, and made our way West. The Compasse varyed 7. degrees from the North to the West. _{margin:} *37. Degrees 25. minutes.*

The sixteenth, faire shining weather, and very hot, the wind variable betweene the North and the West, wee steered away West by North. At noone wee found our height to bee 37. degrees 6. minutes. This morning we sounded and had ground in ninetie fathomes, and in sixe Glasses running it shoalded to fiftie fathoms, and so to eight and twentie fathoms, at foure of the clocke in the after-noone. Then wee came to an Anchor, and rode till eight of the clocke at night, the wind being at South and Moone-light, we resolued to goe to the Northward to finde deeper water. So wee weighed and stood to the Northward, and found the water to shoald and deepe, from eight and twentie to twentie fathomes. _{margin:} *37. Degrees 6. minutes.*

The seuenteenth, faire and cleere Sun-shining weather, the winde at South by West, wee steered to the Northward till foure of the clocke in the morning, then wee came to eighteene fathomes. So we Anchored vntill the Sunne arose to looke abroad for Land, for wee iudged there could not but be Land neere vs, but we could see none. Then we weighed and stood to the Westward till noone. And at eleuen of the clocke wee had sight of a low Land, with a white sandie shoare. By twelue of the clocke we were come into fiue fathomes, and Anchored; and the Land was foure leagues from vs, and wee had sight of it from the West, to the North-west by North. Our height was 37. degrees 26. minutes. Then the wind blew so stiffe a gale, and such a Sea went, that we could not weigh; so we rode there all night an hard rode. _{margin:} *A low Land with a white sandie shoare. 37. degrees 26. minutes.*

The eighteenth, in the morning faire weather, and little winde at North North-east and North-east. At foure of the clocke in the morning, we weighed and stood into the shoare to see the deeping or shoalding of it, and finding it too deepe, we stood in to get a rode; for wee saw as it were three Ilands. So wee turned to windward to get into a Bay, as it shewed to vs to the Westward of an Iland. For the three Ilands did beare North off vs. But toward noone the wind blew Northerly, with gusts of wind and rayne. So we stood off into the Sea againe all night; and running off we found a Channell, wherein we had no lesse then eight, nine, ten, eleuen, and twelue fathomes water. For in comming ouer the Barre, wee had fiue, and foure fathomes and a halfe, and it lyeth fiue leagues from the shoare, and it is the Barre of *Virginia.* At the North end of it, it is ten leagues broad, and South and North, but deepe water from ninetie fathoms to fiue, and foure and a halfe. The Land lyeth South and North. This is the entrance into the *Kings* Riuer in *Virginia*, where our *English*-men are. The North side of it lyeth in 37. degrees 26. minutes, you shall know when you come to shoald water or sounding; for the water will looke Greene or thicke, you shall haue ninetie and eightie fathomes, and shoalding apce till you come to ten, eleuen, nine, eight, seuen, ten, and nine fathomes, and so to fiue, and foure fathomes and a halfe. _{margin:} *Barre of Virginia. Kings Riuer.*

The nineteenth, faire weather, but an hard gale of winde at the North-east, wee stood off till noone, and made our way South-east by East, two and twentie leagues. At noone wee cast about to the Westward, and stood till sixe of the clocke in the after-noone, and went fiue leagues and a halfe North-west by North. Then wee cast about againe to the Eastward, and stood that way till foure the next morning. _{margin:} *Note.*

The twentieth, faire and cleere weather, the winde variable betweene East North-east, and North-east. At foure of the clocke in the morning, wee cast about to the Westward, and stood till noone; at which time I sounded; and had two and thirtie fathomes. Then we takt to the Eastward againe; wee found our height to bee 37. degrees 22. minutes. We stood to the East-ward all night, and had very much wind. At eight of the clocke at night we tooke off our Bonnets, and stood with small sayle. _{margin:} *37. degrees 22. minutes.*

The one and twentieth, was a sore storme of winde and rayne all day and all night, wherefore wee stood to the Eastward with a small sayle : till one of the clocke in the after-noone. Then a great Sea brake into our fore-corse and split it; so we were forced to take it from the yard and mend it ; wee lay a trie with our mayne-corse all night. This night our Cat ranne crying from one side of the ship to the other, looking ouer-boord, which made vs to wonder; but we saw nothing.

E e e

The

The two°and twencieth, ſtormy weather, with guſts of rayne and wind. In the morning at eight of the clocke we ſet our fore-corſe,and ſtood to the Eaſtward vnder our fore-ſayle,mayne-ſayle and miſen, and from noone to noone, we made our way Eaſt South-eaſt, fourteene leagues. The night reaſonable drie but cloudie, the winde variable all day and night. Our Compaſſe was varyed 4.degrees Weſtward.

Variation 4. degrees Weſt-ward.

The three and twentieth, very faire weather, but ſome Thunder in the morning, the winde variable betweene Eaſt by North. At noone wee tackt about to the Northward, the winde at Eaſt by North. The after-noone very faire, the wind variable, and continued ſo all night. Our way we made Eaſt South-eaſt, till noone the next day.

The foure and twentieth,faire and hot weather, with the wind variable betweene the North and the Eaſt. The after-noone variable winde. But at foure of the clocke, the wind came to the Eaſt and South-eaſt ; ſo wee ſteered away North by Weſt, and in three Watches wee went thirteene leagues. At noone our height was 35.degrees 41.minutes, being farre off at Sea from the Land. **10**

The fiue and twentieth, faire weather and very hot. All the morning was very calme vntill eleuen of the clocke ; the wind came to South-eaſt, and South South-eaſt ; ſo wee ſteered away North-weſt by North, two Watches and a halfe, and one Watch North-weſt by Weſt, and went eighteene leagues. At noone I found our height to bee 36.degrees 20.minutes, being without ſight of Land.

The ſixe and twentieth, faire and hot weather, the winde variable vpon all the points of the Compaſſe. From two of the clocke in the morning vntill noone, wee made our way North by Eaſt, ſeuen leagues. In the after-noone the wind came to the North-eaſt, and vering to the Eaſt South-eaſt, wee ſteered away North-weſt fifteene leagues, from noone till ten of the clocke at night. At eight of the clocke at night wee ſounded, and had eighteene fathomes, and were come to the Banke of *Virginia*, and could not ſee the Land. Wee kept ſounding, and ſteered a-way North, and came to eight fathomes, and Anchored there ; for the wind was at Eaſt South-eaſt, ſo that wee could not get off. For the Coaſt lyeth along South South-weſt, and North North-eaſt. At noone our height was 37.degrees 15.minutes. And wee found that we were returned to the ſame place, from whence we were put off at our firſt ſeeing Land. **20**

The Banke of Virginia. The Coaſt lyeth South South-weſt, and North North-weſt. Latitude 37.degrees 15.mi-nutes.

This agreeth with *Robert Tyndall*.

The ſeuen and twentieth, faire weather and very hot, the winde at Eaſt South-eaſt. In the morning as ſoone as the Sunne was vp, wee looked out and had ſight of the Land. Then wee weighed, and ſtood in North-weſt two Glaſſes, and found the Land to bee the place, from whence wee put off firſt. So wee kept our loofe, and ſteered along the Land, and had the Banke lye all along the ſhoare; and wee had in two leagues off the ſhoare,fiue, ſixe, ſeuen, eight, nine,and ten fathomes. The Coaſt lyeth South South-weſt, and is a white Sandie ſhoare, and ſheweth full of Bayes and Points. The ſtreame ſetteth Weſt South-weſt, and Eaſt North-eaſt. At ſixe of the clocke at night, wee were thwart of an Harbour or Riuer, but we ſaw a Barre lye before it ; and all within the Land to the Northward, the water ranne with many Ilands in it. At ſixe of the clocke we Anchored, and ſent our Boate to ſound to the ſhoare-ward, and found no leſſe then foure and a halfe, fiue, ſixe, and ſeuen fathomes. **30**

40

The eight and twentieth, faire and hot weather, the winde at South South-weſt. In the morning at ſixe of the clocke wee weighed, and ſteered away North twelue leagues till noone, and came to the Point of the Land ; and being hard by the Land in fiue fathomes, on a ſud-den wee came into three fathomes ; then we beare vp and had but ten foote water, and ioy-ned to the Point. Then as ſoone as wee were ouer, wee had fiue, ſixe, ſeuen, eight, nine, ten, twelue, and thirteene fathomes. Then wee found the Land to trend away North-weſt, with a great Bay and Riuers. But the Bay wee found ſhoald ; and in the offing wee had ten fathomes, and had ſight of Breaches and drie Sand. Then wee were forced to ſtand backe againe ; ſo we ſtood backe South-eaſt by South, three leagues. And at ſeuen of the clocke wee Anchored in eight fathomes water ; and found a Tide ſet to the North-weſt, and North North-weſt, and it riſeth one fathome, and floweth South South-eaſt. And hee that will throughly Diſ-couer this great Bay, muſt haue a ſmall Pinnaſſe, that muſt draw but foure or fiue foote water, to ſound before him. At fiue in the morning wee weighed, and ſteered away to the Eaſtward on many courſes, for the Norther Land is full of ſhoalds. Wee were among them, and once wee ſtrooke, and wee went away ; and ſteered away to the South-eaſt. So wee had two, three, foure, fiue, ſixe, and ſeuen fathomes, and ſo deeper and deeper. **50**

The Point of the Land.

A great Bay and Riuers.

A ſmall Shal-lop needfull.

The Norther Land is full of ſhoalds.

The nine and twentieth, faire weather, with ſome Thunder and ſhowers, the winde ſhifting betweene the South South-weſt, and the North North-weſt. In the morning wee weighed at the breake of day,and ſtood toward the Norther Land, which we found to bee all Ilands to our ſight, and great ſtormes from them, and are ſhould three leagues off. For we comming by them, had but ſeuen, ſixe, fiue, foure, three, and two fathoms and a halfe, and ſtrooke ground with our Rudder, we ſteered off South-weſt, one Glaſſe, and had fiue fathoms. Then wee ſteered South-eaſt three Glaſſes, then wee found ſeuen fathomes, and ſteered North-eaſt by Eaſt, foure leagues, and came to twelue and thirteene fathoms. At one of the clocke, I went to the top-maſt **60**

Many Ilands.

They ſtrike.

maſt head, and ſet the Land, and the bodie of the Ilands did beare North-weſt by North. And at foure of the clocke , wee had gone foure leagues Eaſt South-eaſt, and North-eaſt by Eaſt, and found but ſeuen fathoms, and it was calme, ſo we Anchored. Then I went againe to the top-maſt head, to ſee how farre I could ſee Land about vs, and could ſee no more but the I-lands. And the Souther point of them did beare North-weſt by Weſt, eight leagues off. So wee rode till mid-night. Then the winde came to the North North-weſt, ſo wee waighed and ſet ſayle.

The thirtieth, in the morning betweene twelue and one, we weighed, and ſtood to the Eaſt-ward, the winde at North North-weſt, wee ſteered away and made our way Eaſt South-eaſt. From our weighing till noone, eleuen leagues. Our ſoundings were eight, nine, ten, eleuen, twelue, and thirteene fathomes till day. Then we came to eighteene, nineteene, twentie, and to ſixe and twentie fathoms by noone. Then I obſerued the Sunne, and found the height to bee 39. degrees 5. minutes, and ſaw no Land. In the after-noone, the winde came to North by Weſt ; So wee lay cloſe by with our fore-ſayle : and our mayne-ſayle, and it was little winde vntill twelue of the clocke at mid-night, then wee had a gale a little while. Then I ſounded, and all the night our ſoundings were thirtie, and ſixe and thirtie fathomes, and wee went little.

Latitude 39. degrees 5. mi-nutes.

The one and thirtieth, faire weather and little wind. At ſixe of the clocke in the morning we caſt about to the Northward, the wind being at the North-eaſt, little wind. At noone it fell calme, and I found the height to bee 38. degrees 39. minutes. And the ſtreames had deceiued vs, and our ſounding was eight and thirtie fathoms. In the afternoone I ſounded againe, and had but thirtie fathoms. So we found that we were heaued too and fro with the ſtreames of the Tide, both by our obſeruations and our depths. From noone till foure of the clocke in the after-noone, it was calme. At ſixe of the clocke wee had a little gale Southerly, and it continued all night, ſometimes calme, and ſometimes a gale ; wee went eight leagues from noone to noone, North by Eaſt.

Latitude 38. degrees 39. mi-nutes. Deceitfull ſtreames.

The firſt of September, faire weather, the wind variable betweene Eaſt and South, we ſteered away North North-weſt. At noone we found our height to bee 39. degrees 3. minutes. Wee had ſoundings thirtie, twentie ſeuen, twentie foure, and twentie two fathomes, as wee went to the Northward. At ſixe of the clocke wee had one and twentie fathomes. And all the third watch till twelue of the clocke at mid-night, we had ſoundings one and twentie, two and twentie, eighteene, two and twentie, one and twentie, eighteene, and two and twentie fathoms, and went ſixe leagues neere hand North North-weſt.

September. Latitude 39. degrees 3. mi-nutes.

The ſecond, in the morning cloſe weather, the winde at South in the morning ; from twelue vntill two of the clocke we ſteered North North-weſt, and had ſounding one and twentie fa-thoms, and in running one Glaſſe we had but ſixteene fathoms, then ſeuenteene, and ſo ſhoalder and ſhoalder vntill it came to twelue fathoms. We ſaw a great Fire, but could not ſee the Land, then we came to ten fathoms, whereupon we brought our tackes aboord, and ſtood to the Eaſt-ward Eaſt South-eaſt, foure Glaſſes. Then the Sunne aroſe, and we ſteered away North againe, and ſaw the Land from the Weſt by North, to the North-weſt by North, all like bro-ken Ilands, and our ſoundings were eleuen and ten fathoms. Then wee looſt in for the ſhoare, and faire by the ſhoare, we had ſeuen fathoms. The courſe along the Land we found to be North-eaſt by North. From the Land which we had firſt ſight of, vntill we came to a great Lake of water, as wee could iudge it to bee, being drowned Land, which made it to riſe like Ilands, which was in length ten leagues. The mouth of that Lake hath many ſhoalds, and the Sea brea-keth on them as it is caſt out of the mouth of it. And from that Lake or Bay, the Land lyeth North by Eaſt, and wee had a great ſtreame out of the Bay ; and from thence our ſounding was ten fathoms, two leagues from the Land. At fiue of the clocke we Anchored, being little winde, and rode in eight fathoms water, the night was faire. This night I found the Land to hall the Compaſſe 8. degrees. For to the Northward off vs we ſaw high Hils. For the day before we found not aboue 2. degrees of Variation. This is a very good Land to fall with, and a plea-ſant Land to ſee.

The Land like broken Ilands. The courſe a-long the Land from the mouth of one Riuer, to the mouth of the Norther Bay or Lake. Variation 8. degrees neere the Hils. 2. degrees va-riation off at Sea.

The third, the morning myſtie vntill ten of the clocke, then it cleered, and the wind came to the South South-eaſt, ſo wee weighed and ſtood to the Northward. The Land is very pleaſant and high, and bold to fall withall. At three of the clocke in the after-noone, wee came to three great Riuers. So we ſtood along to the Northermoſt, thinking to haue gone into it, but we found it to haue a very ſhoald barre before it, for we had but ten foot water. Then wee caſt about to the Southward, and found two fathoms, three fathoms, and three and a quarter, till we came to the Souther ſide of them, then we had fiue and ſixe fathoms, and Anchored. So wee ſent in our Boate to ſound, and they found no leſſe water then foure, fiue, ſixe, and ſeuen fathoms, and re-turned in an houre and a halfe. So wee weighed and went in, and rode in fiue fathoms, Ozie ground, and ſaw many Salmons, and Mullets, and Rayes very great. The height is 40. de-grees 30. minutes.

High and a bold ſhoare. Three great Riuers. The Norther-moſt barred. An excellent Riuer. Latitude 40. degrees 3. mi-nutes.

The fourth, in the morning as ſoone as the day was light, wee ſaw that it was good riding

farther

A very good Harbour.

farther vp. So we fent our Boate to found, and found that it was a very good Harbour ; and foure and fiue fathoms, two Cables length from the fhoare. Then we weighed and went in with our fhip. Then our Boate went on Land with our Net to Fifh, and caught ten great Mullets, of a foot and a halfe long a peece, and a Ray as great as foure men could hale into the fhip. So wee trimmed our Boate and rode ftill all day. At night the wind blew hard at the North-weft, and

The people of the Countrey come aboord, they are very ciuill. Yellow Copper. Tall Oakes.

our Anchor came home, and wee droue on fheare, but tooke no hurt, thanked bee God, for the ground is foft fand and Oze. This day the people of the Countrey came aboord of vs, feeming very glad of our comming, and brought greene Tabacco, and gaue vs of it for Kniues and Beads. They goe in Deere skins loofe, well dreffed. They haue yellow Copper. They defire Cloathes, and are very ciuill. They haue great ftore of Maiz or *Indian* Wheate, whereof they make good Bread. The Countrey is full of great and tall Oakes.   10

The great Bay in 40. degrees and 30. minuts.

The fifth, in the morning as foone as the day was light, the wind ceafed and the Flood came. So we heaued off our fhip againe into fiue fathoms water, and fent our Boate to found the Bay, and we found that there was three fathoms hard by the Souther fhoare. Our men went on Land there, and faw great ftore of Men, Women and Children, who gaue them Tabacco at their com-

Dryed Currants. Mantles of Feathers, Furs, Hempe. Red Copper.

ming on Land. So they went vp into the Woods, and faw great ftore of very goodly Oakes, and fome Currants. For one of them came aboord and brought fome dryed, and gaue me fome, which were fweet and good. This day many of the people came aboord, fome in Mantles of Feathers, and fome in Skinnes of diuers forts of good Furres. Some women alfo came to vs with Hempe. They had red Copper Tabacco pipes, and other things of Copper they did weare about their neckes. At night they went on Land againe, fo wee rode very quiet, but durft not truft them.   20

Another Riuer foure leagues to the North-ward. A narrow Riuer to the Weftward.

The fixth, in the morning was faire weather, and our Mafter fent *Iohn Colman*, with foure other men in our Boate ouer to the North-fide, to found the other Riuer, being foure leagues from vs. They found by the way fhoald water two fathoms : but at the North of the Riuer eighteen, and twentie fathoms, and very good riding for Ships ; and a narrow Riuer to the Weftward betweene two Ilands. The Lands they told vs were as pleafant with Graffe and Flowers, and goodly Trees, as euer they had feene, and very fweet fmells came from them. So they went in two leagues and faw an open Sea, and returned ; and as they came backe, they were fet vpon by two Canoes, the one hauing twelue, the other fourteene men. The night came on, and it began

Colman flaine, and two more hurt.

to rayne, fo that their Match went out ; and they had one man flaine in the fight, which was an *Englifh*-man, named *Iohn Colman*, with an Arrow fhot into his throat, and two more hurt. It grew fo darke that they could not find the fhip that night, but labored too and fro on their Oares. They had fo great a ftreame, that their grapnell would not hold them.   30

Colmans Point.

The feuenth, was faire, and by ten of the clocke they returned aboord the fhip, and brought our dead man with them, whom we carryed on Land and buryed, and named the point after his name, *Colmans* Point. Then we hoyfed in our Boate, and raifed her fide with wafte boords for defence of our men. So we rode ftill all night, hauing good regard to our Watch.

The eight, was very faire weather, wee rode ftill very quietly. The people came aboord vs, and brought Tabacco and *Indian* Wheat, to exchange for Kniues and Beades, and offered vs no violence. So we fitting vp our Boate did marke them, to fee if they would make any fhew of the Death of our man ; which they did not.   40

Treacherous Sauages.

The ninth, faire weather. In the morning, two great Canoes came aboord full of men ; the one with their Bowes and Arrowes, and the other in fhew of buying of Kniues to betray vs ; but we perceiued their intent. Wee tooke two of them that had red Coates on them, and would not fuffer the other to come neere vs. So they went on Land, and two other came aboord in a Canoe : we tooke the one and let the other goe ; but hee which wee had taken, got vp and leapt ouer-boord. Then we weighed and went off into the channell of the Riuer, and Anchored there all night.

The tenth, faire weather, we rode ftill till twelue of the clocke. Then we weighed and went ouer, and found it fhoald all the middle of the Riuer, for wee could finde but two fathoms and a halfe, and three fathomes for the fpace of a league ; then wee came to three fathomes, and foure fathomes, and fo to feuen fathomes, and Anchored, and rode all night in foft Ozie ground. The banke is Sand.   50

Good Harbour

The eleuenth, was faire and very hot weather. At one of the clocke in the after-noone, wee weighed and went into the Riuer, the wind at South South-weft, little winde. Our foundings were feuen, fixe, fiue, fixe, feuen, eight, nine, ten, twelue, thirteene, and fourteene fathomes. Then it fhoalded againe, and came to fiue fathomes. Then wee Anchored, and faw that it was a very good Harbour for all windes, and rode all night. The people of the Countrey came aboord of vs, making fhew of loue, and gaue vs Tabacco and *Indian* Wheat, and departed for that night ; but we durft not truft them.   60

The twelfth, very faire and hot. In the after-noone at two of the clocke wee weighed, the winde being variable, betweene the North and the North-weft. So we turned into the Riuer two leagues and Anchored. This morning at our firft rode in the Riuer, there came eight and

twentie

twentie Canoes full of men, women and children to betray vs : but we saw their intent, and suffered none of them to come aboord of vs. At twelue of the clocke they departed. They brought with them Oysters and Beanes, whereof wee bought some. They haue great Tabacco pipes of yellow Copper, and Pots of Earth to dresse their meate in. It floweth South-east by South within.

28.Canoes full of men.
Oysters and Beanes.
Copper Pipes.

The thirteenth, faire weather, the wind Northerly. At seuen of the clocke in the morning, as the floud came we weighed, and turned foure miles into the Riuer. The tide being done wee anchored. Then there came foure Canoes aboord : but we suffered none of them to come into our ship. They brought great store of very good Oysters aboord, which we bought for trifles.
10 In the night I set the variation of the Compasse, and found it to be 13. degrees. In the afternoone we weighed, and turned in with the floud, two leagues and a halfe further, and anchored all night, and had fiue fathoms soft Ozie ground, and had an high point of Land, which shewed out to vs, bearing North by East fiue leagues off vs.

Variation 13. degrees.

The fourteenth, in the morning being very faire weather, the wind South-east, we sayled vp the Riuer twelue leagues, and had fiue fathoms, and fiue fathoms and a quarter lesse ; and came to a Streight betweene two Points, and had eight, nine, and ten fathoms: and it trended North-east by North, one league : and wee had twelue, thirteene and fourteene fathomes. The Riuer is a mile broad : there is very high Land on both sides. Then wee went vp North-west, a league and an halfe deepe water. Then North-east by North fiue miles ; then North-west
20 by North two leagues, and anchored. The Land grew very high and Mountainous. The Riuer is full of fish.

The Riuer 2 mile broad.
Very high and mountainous Land.

The fifteenth, in the morning was misty vntill the Sunne arose : then it cleered. So wee weighed with the wind at South, and ran vp into the Riuer twentie leagues, passing by high Mountaines. Wee had a very good depth, as sixe, seuen, eight, nine, ten, twelue, and thirteene fathoms, and great store of Salmons in the Riuer. This morning our two Sauages got out of a Port and swam away. After we were vnder sayle, they called to vs in scorne. At night we came to other Mountaines, which lie from the Riuers side. There wee found very louing people, and very old men : where we were well vsed. Our Boat went to fish, and caught great store of very good fish.

Very louing people.

30 The sixteenth, faire and very hot weather. In the morning our Boat went againe to fishing, but could catch but few, by reason their Canoes had beene there all night. This morning the people came aboord, and brought vs eares of *Indian* Corne, and Pompions, and Tabacco: which wee bought for trifles. Wee rode still all day, and filled fresh water ; at night wee weighed and went two leagues higher, and had shoald water : so wee anchored till day.

Maiz, Pompions and Tabacco.

The seuenteenth, faire Sun-shining weather, and very hot. In the morning as soone as the Sun was vp, we set sayle, and ran vp sixe leagues higher, and found shoalds in the middle of the channell, and small Ilands, but seuen fathoms water on both sides. Toward night we borrowed so neere the shoare, that we grounded : so we layed out our small anchor, and heaued off againe. Then we borrowed on the banke in the channell, and came aground againe ; while the floud ran
40 we heaued off againe, and anchored all night.

Shoalds and small Ilands.

The eighteenth, in the morning was faire weather, and we rode still. In the after-noone our Masters Mate went on land with an old Sauage, a Gouernour of the Countrey; who carried him to his house, and made him good cheere. The nineteenth, was faire and hot weather: at the floud being neere eleuen of the clocke, wee weighed, and ran higher vp two leagues aboue the Shoalds, and had no lesse water then fiue fathoms : wee anchored, and rode in eight fathomes. The people of the Countrie came flocking aboord, and brought vs Grapes, and Pompions, which wee bought for trifles. And many brought vs Beuers skinnes, and Otters skinnes, which wee bought for Beades, Kniues, and Hatchets. So we rode there all night.

Grapes and Pompions : Beuers and Otters skins.

The twentieth, in the morning was faire weather. Our Masters Mate with foure men more
50 went vp with our Boat to sound the Riuer, and found two leagues aboue vs but two fathomes water, and the channell very narrow ; and aboue that place seuen or eight fathomes. Toward night they returned : and we rode still all night. The one and twentieth, was faire weather, and the wind all Southerly : we determined yet once more to goe farther vp into the Riuer, to trie what depth and breadth it did beare ; but much people resorted aboord, so wee went not this day. Our Carpenter went on land, and made a Fore-yard. And our Master and his Mate determined to trie some of the chiefe men of the Countrey, whether they had any treacherie in them. So they tooke them downe into the Cabbin, and gaue them so much Wine and *Aqua vita*, that they were all merrie : and one of them had his wife with him, which sate so modestly, as any of our Countrey women would doe in a strange place. In the end one of them was
60 drunke, which had beene aboord of our ship all the time that we had beene there: and that was strange to them ; for they could not tell how to take it. The Canoes and folke went all on shoare: but some of them came againe, and brought stropes of Beades : some had sixe, seuen, eight, nine, ten ; and gaue him. So he slept all night quietly.

The two and twentieth, was faire weather : in the morning our Masters Mate and foure more

of the companie went vp with our Boat to ſound the Riuer higher vp. The people of the Countrey came not aboord till noone : but when they came, and ſaw the Sauages well, they were
glad. So at three of the clocke in the after-noone they came aboord, and brought Tabacco, and

Oration. more Beades, and gaue them to our Maſter, and made an Oration, and ſhewed him all the Countrey round about. Then they ſent one of their companie on land, who preſently returned, and
brought a great Platter full of Veniſon, dreſſed by themſelues ; and they cauſed him to eate with
them : then they made him reuerence, and departed all ſaue the old man that lay aboord. This
night at ten of the clocke, our Boat returned in a ſhowre of raine from ſounding of the Riuer ;

End of the Ri- and found it to bee at an end for ſhipping to goe in. For they had beene vp eight or nine leagues,
uers Nauiga- and found but ſeuen foot water, and vnconſtant ſoundings.   10
blenesse.

They returne The three and twentieth, faire weather. At twelue of the clocke wee weighed, and went
downe the downe two leagues to a ſhoald that had two channels, one on the one ſide, and another on the
Riuer. other, and had little wind, whereby the tide layed vs vpon it. So, there wee ſate on ground the
ſpace of an houre till the floud came. Then we had a little gale of wind at the Weſt. So wee
got our ſhip into deepe water, and rode all night very well.

The foure and twentieth was faire weather : the winde at the North-weſt, wee weighed,
and went downe the Riuer ſeuen or eight leagues ; and at halfe ebbe wee came on ground on a
banke of Oze in the middle of the Riuer, and ſate there till the floud. Then wee went on

Store of Cheſt- Land, and gathered good ſtore of Cheſt-nuts. At ten of the clocke wee came off into deepe
nuts. water, and anchored.   20

The fiue and twentieth was faire weather, and the wind at South a ſtiffe gale. We rode ſtill,
and went on Land to walke on the Weſt ſide of the Riuer, and found good ground for Corne,

Okes, Wal-nut and other Garden herbs, with great ſtore of goodly Oakes, and Wal-nut trees, and Cheſt-nut
trees, Cheſt- trees, Ewe trees, and trees of ſweet wood in great abundance, and great ſtore of Slate for houſes,
nut trees, Ewe and other good ſtones.
trees, Cedar
trees, &c. The ſixe and twentieth was faire weather, and the wind at South a ſtiffe gale, wee rode ſtill.
In the morning our Carpenter went on Land with our Maſters Mate, and foure more of our
companie to cut wood. This morning, two Canoes came vp the Riuer from the place where we
firſt found louing people, and in one of them was the old man that had lyen aboord of vs at the
other place. He brought another old man with him, which brought more ſtropes of Beades, and 30
gaue them to our Maſter, and ſhewed him all the Countrey there about, as though it were at his
command. So he made the two old men dine with him, and the old mans wife : for they brought
two old women, and two young maidens of the age of ſixteene or ſeuenteene yeeres with them,
who behaued themſelues very modeſtly. Our Maſter gaue one of the old men a Knife, and they
gaue him and vs Tabacco. And at one of the clocke they departed downe the Riuer, making
ſignes that wee ſhould come downe to them ; for wee were within two leagues of the place
where they dwelt.

The ſeuen and twentieth, in the morning was faire weather, but much wind at the North,
we weighed and ſet our fore top-ſayle, and our ſhip would not flat, but ran on the Ozie banke
at halfe ebbe. Wee layed out anchor to heaue her off, but could not. So wee ſate from halfe 40
ebbe to halfe floud : then wee ſet our fore-ſayle and mayne top-ſayle, and got downe ſixe
leagues. The old man came aboord, and would haue had vs anchor, and goe on Land to eate with
him : but the wind being faire, we would not yeeld to his requeſt ; So hee left vs, being very
ſorrowfull for our departure. At fiue of the clocke in the after-noone, the wind came to the
South South-weſt. So wee made a boord or two, and anchored in fourteene fathomes water.
Then our Boat went on ſhoare to fiſh right againſt the ſhip. Our Maſters Mate and Boat-ſwaine,
and three more of the companie went on land to fiſh, but could not finde a good place. They
tooke foure or fiue and twentie Mullets, Breames, Baſes, and Barbils ; and returned in an houre.
We rode ſtill all night.

The eight and twentieth, being faire weather, as ſoone as the day was light, wee weighed at 50
halfe ebbe, and turned downe two leagues belowe water ; for, the ſtreame doth runne the laſt
quarter ebbe : then we anchored till high water. At three of the clocke in the after-noone we
weighed, and turned downe three leagues, vntill it was darke : then wee anchored.

The nine and twentieth was drie cloſe weather : the wind at South, and South and by Weſt,
we weighed early in the morning, and turned downe three leagues by a lowe water, and anchored at the lower end of the long Reach ; for it is ſixe leagues long. Then there came certaine
Indians in a Canoe to vs, but would not come aboord. After dinner there came the Canoe with
other men, whereof three came aboord vs. They brought *Indian* Wheat, which wee bought
for trifles. At three of the clocke in the after-noone wee weighed, as ſoone as the ebbe came,

Mountaines. and turned downe to the edge of the Mountaines, or the Northermoſt of the Mountaines, and 60
anchored : becauſe the high Land hath many Points, and a narrow channell, and hath many
eddie winds. So we rode quietly all night in ſeuen fathoms water.

The thirtieth was faire weather, and the wind at South-eaſt a ſtiffe gale betwene the Mountaynes. We rode ſtill the after-noone. The people of the Countrey came aboord vs, and brought

ſome

some small skinnes with them, which we bought for Kniues and Trifles. This a very pleasant *Small skins.* place to build a Towne on. The Road is very neere, and very good for all winds, saue an East *A pleasant* North-east wind. The Mountaynes looke as if some Metall or Minerall were in them. For the *place to build* Trees that grow on them were all blasted, and some of them barren with few or no Trees on *a Towne on.* them. The people brought a stone aboord like to Emery (a stone vsed by Glasiers to cut Glasse) it would cut Iron or Steele: Yet being bruised small, and water put to it, it made a colour like *Likelihood of* blacke Lead glistering; It is also good for Painters Colours. At three of the clocke they depar- *Minerals.* ted, and we rode still all night.

The first of October, faire weather, the wind variable betweene the West and the North. In *October.* 10 the morning we weighed at seuen of the clocke with the ebbe, and got downe below the Mountaynes, which was seuen leagues. Then it fell calme and the floud was come, and wee anchored at twelue of the clocke. The people of the Mountaynes came aboord vs, wondring at our ship and weapons. We bought some small skinnes of them for Trifles. This after-noone, one Canoe kept hanging vnder our sterne with one man in it, which we could not keepe from thence, who got vp by our Rudder to the Cabin window, and stole out my Pillow, and two Shirts, and two Bandeleeres. Our Masters Mate shot at him, and strooke him on the brest, and killed him. Whereupon all the rest fled away, some in their Canoes, and so leapt out of them into the water. We manned our Boat, and got our things againe. Then one of them that swamme got hold of our Boat, thinking to ouerthrow it. But our Cooke tooke a Sword, and cut off one of his hands, and 20 he was drowned. By this time the ebbe was come, and we weighed and got downe two leagues, by that time it was darke. So we anchored in foure fathomes water, and rode well.

The second, faire weather. At breake of day wee weighed, the wind being at North-west, and got downe seuen leagues; then the floud was come strong, so we anchored. Then came one of the Sauages that swamme away from vs at our going vp the Riuer with many other, thinking *Treacherie of* to betray vs. But wee perceiued their intent, and suffered none of them to enter our ship. *these Sauages.* Whereupon two Canoes full of men, with their Bowes and Arrowes shot at vs after our sterne: *A skirmish and* in recompence whereof we discharged sixe Muskets, and killed two or three of them. Then a- *slaughter of* boue an hundred of them came to a point of Land to shoot at vs. There I shot a Falcon at them, *the Sauages.* and killed two of them: whereupon the rest fled into the Woods. Yet they manned off another 30 Canoe with nine or ten men, which came to meet vs. So I shot at it also a Falcon, and shot it through, and killed one of them. Then our men with their Muskets, killed three or foure more of them. So they went their way, within a while after, wee got downe two leagues beyond that place, and anchored in a Bay, cleere from all danger of them on the other side of the Riuer, where we saw a very good piece of ground: and hard by it there was a Cliffe, that looked of the *A Myne of* colour of a white greene, as though it were either Copper, or Siluer Myne: and I thinke it to be *Copper or* one of them, by the Trees that grow vpon it. For they be all burned, and the other places are *Siluer.* greene as grasse, it is on that side of the Riuer that is called *Manna-hata*. There we saw no peo- *The Countrey* ple to trouble vs: and rode quietly all night, but had much wind and raine. *of Manna-hata;*

The third, was very stormie; the wind at East North-east. In the morning, in a gust of wind 40 and raine our Anchor came home, and we droue on ground, but it was Ozie. Then as we were about to haue out an Anchor, the wind came to the North North-west, and droue vs off againe. Then we shot an Anchor, and let it fall in foure fathomes water, and weighed the other. Wee had much wind and raine, with thicke weather: so we roade still all night.

The fourth, was faire weather, and the wind at North North-west, wee weighed and came out of the Riuer, into which we had runne so farre. Within a while after, wee came out also of *The great mouth of the great Riuer*, that runneth vp to the North-west, borrowing vpon the *The great mouth* Norther side of the same, thinking to haue deepe water: for wee had sounded a great way with *of the great Ri-* our Boat at our first going in, and found seuen, six, and fiue fathomes. So we came out that way, *uer.* but we were deceiued, for we had but eight foot & an halfe water: and so to three, fiue, three, and 50 two fathomes and an halfe. And then three, foure, fiue, sixe, seuen, eight, nine and ten fathomes. And by twelue of the clocke we were cleere of all the Inlet. Then we tooke in our Boat, and set *They leaue* our mayne-sayle and sprit-sayle, and our top-sayles, and steered away East South-east, and *the Coast of* South-east by East off into the mayne sea: and the Land on the Souther-side of the Bay or In- *Virginia.* let, did beare at noone West and by South foure leagues from vs.

The fift, was faire weather, and the wind variable betweene the North and the East. Wee held on our course South-east by East. At noone I obserued and found our height to bee 39. degrees 30. minutes. Our Compasse varied sixe degrees to the West.

We continued our course toward *England*, without seeing any Land by the way, all the rest of this moneth of October: And on the seuenth day of Nouember, *stilo nouo*, being Satur- 60 day: by the Grace of God we safely arriued in the Range of *Dartmouth* in *Deuonshire*, in the yeere 1609.

CHAP.

CHAP. XVII.

An Abstract of the Iournall of MASTER HENRY HVDSON, *for the Discouerie of the North-west Passage, begunne the seuenteenth of A-prill,* 1610. *ended with his end, being treacherously exposed by some of the Companie.*

April 17.

He seuenteenth of Aprill, 1610. we brake ground, and went downe from Saint Katharines Poole, and fell downe to *Blacks-wall*: and so plyed downe with the 10 ships to *Lee*, which was the two and twentieth day.

The two and twentieth, I caused Master *Coleburne* to bee put into a Pinke, bound for *London*, with my Letter to the Aduenturers, importing the reason wherefore I so put him out of the ship, and so plyed forth.

May. The second of May, the wind Southerly, at Eeuen we were thwart of *Flamborough* Head.

The Iles of Orkney.
The fift, we were at the Iles of *Orkney*, and here I set the North end of the Needle, and the North of the Flie all one.

The sixt, wee were in the latitude of 59. degrees 22. minutes, and there perceiued that the North end of *Scotland*, *Orney*, and *Shotland* are not so Northerly, as is commonly set downe.

Note. Farre Ilands 61 degrees 24. minutes. Weßmony.
The eight day, wee saw *Farre* Ilands, in the latitude of 62. degrees 24. minutes. The eleuenth 20 day, we fell with the Easter part of *Isand*, and then plying along the Souther part of the Land, we came to *Weßmony*, being the fifteenth day, and still plyed about the mayne Iland, vntill the last of May with contrary winds, and we got some Fowles of diuers sorts.

Iune.
The first day of Iune, we put to Sea out of an Harbour, in the Westermost part of *Isand*, and so plyed to the Westward in the latitude of 66. degrees 34. minutes, and the second day plyed and found our selues in 65. degrees 57. minutes, with little wind Easterly.

The third day, wee found our selues in 65. degrees 30. minutes, with winde at North-east, a little before this we sayled neere some Ice.

Groneland.
The fourth day, we saw *Groneland* ouer the Ice perfectly, and this night the Sunne went downe due North, and rose North North-east. So plying the fift day, we were in 65. degrees, 30 still encombred with much Ice, which hung vpon the Coast of *Groneland*.

Frobishers Streights.
The ninth day, wee were off *Frobishers* Streights with the winde Northerly, and plyed vnto the South-westwards vntill the fifteenth day.

Desolation.
The fifteenth day, we were in sight of the land, in latitude 59. degrees 27. minutes, which was called by Captayne *Iohn Dauis, Desolation,* and found the errour of the former laying downe of that Land: and then running to the North-westward vntill the twentieth day, wee found the ship in 60. degrees 42. minutes, and saw much Ice, and many Riplings or Ouer-fals, and a strong

A current West North-west.
streame setting from East South-east, to West North-west.

The one and twentie, two and twentie, and three and twentie dayes, with the winde variable, we plyed to the North-westward in sight of much Ice, into the height of 62. degrees 40 29. minutes.

East entrance into the Streights.
The foure and twentie, and fiue and twentie dayes, sayling to the West-ward about midnight, wee saw Land North, which was suddenly lost againe. So wee ranne still to the Westward in 62. degrees 17. minutes.

Iuly.
The fift of Iuly, wee plyed vp vpon the Souther side, troubled with much Ice in seeking the shoare vntill the fift day of Iuly, and we obserued that day in 59. degrees 16. minntes. Then we plyed off the shoare againe, vntill the eight day, and then found the height of the Pole in 60. degrees no minutes. Here we saw the Land from the North-west by West, halfe Norther-

Desire prouoketh.
ly vnto the South-west by West, couered with snow, a Champaigne Land, and called it, *Desire prouoketh.*

We still plyed vp to the Westward, as the Land and Ice would suffer vntill the eleuenth day; 50 when fearing a storme, we anchored by three Rockie Ilands in vncertayne depth, betweene two and nine fathomes; and found it an Harbour vnsufficient by reason of sunken Rockes, one of

Iles of Gods Mercies.
which was next morning two fathomes aboue water. Wee called them the *Iles of Gods Mercies.* The water floweth here better then foure fathomes. The Floud commeth from the North, flowing eight the change day. The latitude in this place is 62. degrees 9. minutes. Then plying to the South-westward the sixteenth day, wee were in the latitude of 58. degrees 50. minutes, but found our selues imbayed with Land, and had much Ice: and we plyed to the North-westward vntill the nineteenth day, and then wee found by obseruation the height of the Pole in 61. degrees 24. minutes, and saw the Land, which I na- 60

Hold with Hope. A mightie growne Sea.
med, *Hold with Hope.* Hence I plyed to the North-westward still, vntill the one and twentieth day, with the wind variable. Heere I found the Sea more growne, then any wee had since wee left *England.*

The three and twentieth day, by obseruation the height of the Pole was 61. degrees 33. minutes,

The fiue and twentieth day, we ſaw the Land; and named it *Magna Britannia*. The ſixe and twentieth day, wee obſerued and found the latitude in 62. degrees 44. minutes. The eight and twentieth day, we were in the height of 63. degrees 10. minutes, and plyed Southerly of the Weſt. The one and thirtieth day, plying to the Weſtward, at noone wee found our ſelues in 62. degrees 24. minutes. *Magna Britannia.*

The firſt of Auguſt, we had ſight of the Northerne ſhoare, from the North by Eaſt to the Weſt by South off vs: the North part twelue leagues, and the Weſter part twentie leagues from vs: and we had no ground there at one hundred and eightie fathomes. And I thinke I ſaw Land on the Sunne ſide, but could not make it perfectly, bearing Eaſt North-eaſt. Here I found the latitude 62. degrees 50. minutes. *Auguſt.*

The ſecond day, we had ſight of a faire Head-land, on the Norther ſhoare ſix leagues off, which I called *Saliſburies* Fore-land : we ranne from them Weſt South-weſt, fourteene leagues : In the mid-way of which wee were ſuddenly come into a great and whurling Sea, whether cauſed by meeting of two ſtreames, or an Ouer-fall, I know not. Thence ſayling Weſt and by South ſeuen leagues farther, we were in the mouth of a Streight and ſounded, and had no ground at one hundred fathomes : the Streight being there not aboue two leagues broad, in the paſſage in this Weſter part : which from the Eaſter part of *Fretum Danis*, is diſtant two hundred and fiftie leagues there abouts. *Saliſburies fore-land; A great and whurling Seas A Streight which led vs into the deepe Bay of Gods great Mercies.*

The third day, we put through the narrow paſſage, after our men had beene on Land, which had well obſerued there, *That the Floud did come from the North*, flowing by the ſhoare fiue fathomes. The head of this entrance on the South ſide, I named Cape *Worſenholme*; and the head on the North-weſter ſhoare, I called Cape *Digs.* After wee had ſailed with an Eaſterly winde, Weſt and by South ten leagues, the Land fell away to the Southward, and the other Iles and Land left vs to the Weſtward. Then I obſerued and found the ſhip at noone in 61. degrees 20. minutes, and a Sea to the Weſtward. *Cape Worſenholme. Cape Digs.*

A larger Diſcourſe of the ſame Voyage, and the ſucceſſe thereof, written by ABACVK PRICKET.

WE began our Voyage for the North-weſt paſſage; the ſeuenteenth of Aprill, 1610. Thwart of *Sheper*, our Maſter ſent Maſter *Colbert* backe to the Owners with his Letter. The next day we weighed from hence, and ſtood for *Harwich*, and came thither the eight and twentieth of Aprill. From *Harwich* we ſet ſayle the firſt of May, along the Coaſt to the North, till we came to the Iles of *Orkney*, from thence to the Iles of *Faro*, and from thence to *Iſland :* on which we fell in a fogge, hearing the Rut of the Sea aſhoare, but ſaw not the Land whereupon our Maſter came to an Anchor. Heere we were embayed in the South-eaſt part of the Land. Wee weighed and ſtood along the Coaſt, on the Weſt ſide towards the North : but one day being calme, we fell a fiſhing, and caught good ſtore of fiſh, as Cod and Ling, and Butte, with ſome other ſorts that we knew not. The next day, we had a good gale of wind at South-weſt, and rayſed the Iles of *Weſtmonie*, where the King of *Denmarke* hath a Fortreſſe, by which we paſſed to rayſe the *Snow Hill* foot, a Mountayne ſo called on the North-weſt part of the Land. But in our courſe we ſaw that famous Hill, Mount *Hecla*, which caſt out much fire, a ſigne of foule weather to come in ſhort time. Wee leaue *Iſland* a ſterne of vs, and met a Mayne of Ice, which did hang on the North part of *Iſland*, and ſtretched downe to the Weſt, which when our Maſter ſaw, he ſtood backe for *Iſland* to find an Harbour, which we did on the North-weſt part, called * *Dereſer*, where wee killed good ſtore of Fowle. From hence wee put to Sea againe, but (neither wind nor weather ſeruing) our Maſter ſtood backe for this Harbour againe, but could not reach it; but fell with another to the South of that, called by our Engliſhmen, *Louſie* Bay : where on the ſhoare we found an hot Bath, and heere all our Engliſhmen bathed themſelues : the water was ſo hot that it would ſcald a Fowle. *Orkney. Farre Iles. Iſland. The South-eaſt part of Iſland. Weſtmonie Iland. Mount Hecla caſteth out fire. A mayne of Ice.* *Or Diraford. Louſie Bay. An hot Bath.*

From hence the firſt of Iune we put to Sea for *Groneland*, but to the Weſt wee ſaw Land as we thought, for which we beare the beſt part of a day, but it proued but a foggie banke. So wee gaue it ouer, and made for *Gronland*, which we rayſed the fourth of Iune. Vpon the Coaſt thereof hung good ſtore of Ice, ſo that our Maſter could not attayne to the ſhoare by any meanes. The Land in this part is very Mountaynous, and full of round Hils, like to Sugar-loaues, couered with ſnow. We turned the Land on the South ſide, as neere as the Ice would ſuffer vs. Our courſe for the moſt part was betweene the Weſt and North-weſt, till we rayſed the *Deſolations*, which is a great Iland in the Weſt part of *Groneland*. On this Coaſt we ſaw ſtore of Whales, and at one time three of them came cloſe by vs, ſo as wee could hardly ſhunne them : then two paſſing very neere, and the third going vnder our ſhip, wee receiued no harme by them, prayſed bee God. *The firſt of Iune. Iland of Deſolation. Store of Whales.*

From the *Deſolations* our Maſter made his way North-weſt, the wind being againſt him, who elſe

elfe would haue gone more to the North : but in this courfe we faw the firft great Iland or Mountayne of Ice, whereof after we faw ftore. About the latter end of Iune, we rayfed Land to the
North of vs, which our Mafter tooke to bee that Iland which Mafter *Danis* fetteth downe in
his Chart. On the Weft fide of his Streight, our Mafter would haue gone to the North of it,
but the wind would not fuffer him : fo we fell to the South of it, into a great Rippling or ouer-
fall of current, the which fetteth to the Weft. Into the current we went, and made our way to
the North of the Weft, till we met with Ice which hung on this Iland. Wherefore our Mafter cafting about, cleered himfelfe of this Ice, and ftood to the South, and then to the Weft,
through ftore of floting Ice, and vpon the Ice ftore of Seales. We gained a cleere Sea, and continued our courfe till wee meete Ice; firft, with great Ilands, and then with ftore of the fmaller   10
fort. Betweene them we made our courfe North-weft, till we met with Ice againe. But, in this
our going betweene the Ice, we faw one of the great Ilands of Ice ouerturne, which was a good

*Iland of Ice o-
uerturneth.*

warning to vs, not to come nigh them, nor within their reach. Into the Ice wee put ahead, as
betweene two Lands. The next day we had a ftorme, and the wind brought the Ice fo faft vpon
vs, that in the end we were driuen to put her into the chiefeft of the Ice, and there to let her lie.
Some of our men this day fell ficke, I will not fay it was for feare, although I faw fmall figne of
other griefe.

Danger by Ice.

The ftorme ceafing, we ftood out of the Ice, where wee faw any cleere Sea to goe to : which
was fometime more, and fometime leffe. Our courfe was as the Ice did lye, fometime to the
North, then to the North-weft, and then to the Weft, and to the South-weft : but ftill inclo-   20
fed with Ice. Which when our Mafter faw, he made his courfe to the South, thinking to cleere
himfelfe of the Ice that way : but the more he ftroue, the worfe he was, and the more inclofed,
till we could goe no further. Here our Mafter was in defpaire, and (as he told me after) he thought
he fhould neuer haue got out of this Ice, but there haue perifhed. Therefore hee brought forth
his Card, and fhewed all the company, that hee was entred aboue an hundred leagues further

*Hudfon entred
100. leagues
further then
any had been.*

then euer any *Englifh* was : and left it to their choice, whether they would proceed any further;
yea, or nay. Whereupon, fome were of one minde, and fome of another, fome wifhing themfelues at home, and fome not caring where, fo they were out of the Ice : but there were fome
who then fpake words, which were remembred a great while after.

Difcontents.

There was one who told the Mafter, that if he had an hundred pounds, hee would giue foure-   30
fcore and ten to be at home : but the Carpenter made anfwere, that if hee had an hundred, hee
would not giue ten vpon any fuch condition, but would thinke it to be as good money as euer he
had any, and to bring it as well home, by the leaue of God. After many words to no purpofe,
to worke we muft on all hands, to get our felues out, and to cleere our fhip. After much labour
and time fpent, we gained roome to turne our fhip in, and fo by little and little, to get cleere in
the Sea a league or two off, our courfe being North and North-weft.

In the end, we rayfed Land to the South-weft, high Land and couered with Snow. Our Ma-

Defire prouokes.

fter named this Land, *Defire prouokes.* Lying here, wee heard the noyfe of a great ouer-fall of a
tyde, that came out of the Land : for now we might fee well, that wee had beene embayed before, and time had made vs know, being fo well acquainted with the Ice, that when night, or   40
foggie, or foule weather tooke vs, we would feeke out the broadeft Iland of Ice, and there come
to anchor and runne, and fport, and fill water that ftood on the Ice in Ponds, both fweete and

*Exercifes of
pleafure and
profit on the
Ice.
Difference of
Tydes and
Bayes.
Ice aboue 100.
fathome.*

good. But after we had brought this Land to beare South of vs, we had the tyde and the current to open the Ice, as being carried firft one way, and then another : but in Bayes they lye as
in a pond without mouing. In this Bay where wee were thus troubled with Ice, wee faw many
of thofe Mountaynes of Ice aground, in fixe or feuenfcore fathome water. In this our courfe we
faw a Beare vpon a piece of Ice by it felfe, to the which our men gaue chafe with their Boat :
but before they came nigh her, the tyde had carried the Ice and the Beare on it, and ioyned
it with the other Ice : fo they loft their labour, and came aboord againe.

We continued our courfe to the North-weft, and rayfed Land to the North of our courfe, to-   50
ward which we made, and comming nigh it, there hung on the Eaftermoft point, many Ilands
of floting Ice, and a Beare on one of them, which from one to another came towards vs, till fhe
was readie to come aboord. But when fhe faw vs looke at her, fhe caft her head betweene her hinder legges, and then diued vnder the Ice : and fo from one piece to another, till fhe was out of our
reach. We ftood along by the Land on the Southfide ahead of vs, wee met with Ice that hung
on a point of Land that lay to the South, more then this that we came vp by : which when our

*A dangerous
Rocke.*

Mafter faw, he ftood in for the fhoare. At the Weft end of this Iland (for fo it is) we found an
Harbour, and came in (at a full Sea) ouer a Rocke, which had two fathome and an halfe on it,
and was fo much bare at a low water. But by the great mercie of God, we came to an Anchor

*Iles of Gods
Mercie.*

cleere of it : and clofe by it, our Mafter named them, the *Iles of Gods Mercie.* This is an Har-   60
bour for need, but there muft be care had how they come in. Heere our Mafter fent me, and o-
thers with me, to difcouer to the North and North-weft : and in going from one place to another, we fprung a Couey of Partridges which were young : at the which *Thomas Woodhoufe*

Partridges.

fhot, but killed only the old one. This Iland is a moft barren place, hauing nothing on it but

plafhes

plaſhes of water and riuen Rockes, as if it were ſubieƈt to Earthquakes. To the North there is a great Bay, or Sea (for I know not what it will proue) where I ſaw a great Iland of Ice aground, betweene the two Lands, which with the Spring-tide was ſet afloat, and carried into this Bay or Sea to the North-weſtward, but came not backe againe, nor within ſight. Here wee tooke in ſome Drift wood that we found aſhoare.

Drift-wood.

From hence we ſtood to the South-weſt, to double the Land to the Weſt of vs, through much floting Ice: In the end wee found a cleere Sea, and continued therein, till wee rayſed Land to the North-weſt. Then our Maſter made his courſe more to the South then before: but it was not long ere we met with Ice which lay ahead of vs. Our Maſter would haue doubled this Ice to the North, but could not; and in the end put into it downe to the South-weſt through much Ice, and then to the South, where we were embayed againe. Our Maſter ſtroue to get the ſhoare, but could not, for the great ſtore of Ice that was on the coaſt. From out of this Bay, we ſtood to the North, and were ſoone out of the Ice: then downe to the South-weſt, and ſo to the Weſt, where we were encloſed (to our ſight) with Land and Ice. For wee had Land from the South to the North-weſt on one ſide, and from the Eaſt to the Weſt on the other: but the Land that was to the North of vs, and lay by Eaſt and Weſt, was but an Iland. On we went till we could goe no further for Ice: ſo we made our ſhip faſt to the Ice which the tide brought vpon vs, but when the ebbe came, the Ice did open, and made way; ſo as in ſeuen or eight houres we were cleere from the Ice, till we came to weather; but onely ſome of the great Ilands, that were carried along with vs to the North-weſt.

Hauing a cleere Sea, our Maſter ſtood to the Weſt along by the South ſhoare, and rayſed three Capes or Head-lands, lying one aboue another. The middlemoſt is an Iland, and maketh a Bay or Harbour, which (I take) will proue a good one. Our Maſter named them Prince *Henries* Cape, or *Fore-land.* When we had layd this we raiſed another, which was the extreme point of the Land, looking towards the North: vpon it are two Hills, but one (aboue the reſt) like an Hay-cocke; which our Maſter named, King *Iames* his Cape. To the North of this, lie certaine Ilands, which our Maſter named, Queene *Annes* Cape, or *Fore-land.* Wee followed the North ſhoare ſtill. Beyond the Kings Cape there is a Sound or Bay, that hath ſome Ilands in it: and this is not to be forgotten, if need be. Beyond this, lieth ſome broken Land, cloſe to the Mayne, but what it is I know not: becauſe we paſſed by it in the night.

Three Capes.
Prince Henries Cape.
King Iames his Cape.
Queene Annes Cape.

Wee ſtood to the North to double this Land, and after to the Weſt againe, till wee fell with Land that ſtretched from the Mayne, like a ſhewer from the South to the North, and from the North to the Weſt, and then downe to the South againe. Being ſhort of this Land, a ſtorme tooke vs, the wind at Weſt, we ſtood to the North, and raiſed Land: which when our Maſter ſaw, he ſtood to the South againe; for he was loath at any time that wee ſhould ſee the North ſhoare. The ſtorme continuing, and comming to the South ſhoare againe, our Maſter found himſelfe ſhot to the Weſt, a great way, which made him muſe, conſidering his Leeward way. To the South-weſt of this Land, on the Mayne, there is an high Hill, which our Maſter named Mount *Charles.* To the North and beyond this, lieth an Iland, that to the Eaſt hath a faire head, and beyond it to the Weſt other broken Land, which maketh a Bay within, and a good Road may be found there for ſhips. Our Maſter named the firſt, Cape *Salſburie.*

Note.

Mount Charles.

Cape Salsburie.

When we had left this to the North-eaſt, we fell into a Rippling or Ouer-fall of a Current, which (at the firſt we tooke to bee a Shoald: but the Lead being caſt, wee had no ground. On we paſſed ſtill in ſight of the South ſhoare, till we raiſed Land lying from the Mayne ſome two leagues. Our Maſter tooke this to bee a part of the Mayne of the North Land; but it is an Iland, the North ſide ſtretching out to the Weſt more then the South. This Iland hath a faire Head to the Eaſt, and very high Land, which our Maſter named *Deepes* Cape: and the Land on the South ſide, now falling away to the South, makes another Cape or Head-land, which our Maſter named, *Worſenhams* Cape. When wee were nigh the North or Iland Cape, our Maſter ſent the Boat aſhoare, with my ſelfe (who had the charge) and the Carpenter, and diuers others, to diſcouer to the Weſt and North-weſt, and to the South-weſt: but we had further to it then we thought; for the Land is very high, and we were ouer-taken with a ſtorme of Raine, Thunder and Lightning. But to it we came on the North-eaſt ſide, and vp we got from one Rocke to another, till we came to the higheſt of that part. Here we found ſome plaine ground, and ſaw ſome Deere; as firſt, foure or fiue, and after, a dozen or ſixteene in an Herd, but could not come nigh them with a Musket ſhot.

Deepes Cape.
Worſenhams Cape.

Deere.

Thus, going from one place to another, wee ſaw to the Weſt of vs an high Hill aboue all the reſt, it being nigh vs: but it proued further off then we made account; for, when wee came to it, the Land was ſo ſteepe on the Eaſt and North-eaſt parts, that wee could not get vnto it. To the South-weſt we ſaw ſome might, and towards that part wee went along by the ſide of a great Pond of water, which lieth vnder the Eaſt ſide of this Hill: and there runneth out of it a ſtreame of water, as much as would driue an ouer-ſhot Mill; which falleth downe from an high Cliffe into the Sea on the South ſide. In this place great ſtore of Fowle breed, and there is the beſt Graſſe that I had ſeene ſince we came from *England.* Here wee found Sorell, and that

Store of fowle and graſſe.
Sorell and Scuruy graſſe.

which

which wee call Scuruy-graſſe, in great abundance. Paſſing along wee ſaw ſome round Hills of ſtone, like to Graſſe cockes, which at the firſt I tooke to be the worke of ſome Chriſtian. Wee paſſed by them, till we came to the South ſide of the Hill ; we went vnto them, and there found more ; and being nigh them, I turned off the vppermoſt ſtone, and found them hollow within, **Fowles han-** and full of Fowles hanged by their neckes. Then   *Greene*, and I, went to fetch the Boat to **ged.** the South ſide, while *Robert Billet* and hee got downe a Valley to the Sea ſide, where wee tooke them in.

Our Maſter (in this time) came in betweene the two Lands, and ſhot off ſome Peeces to call vs aboord ; for it was a fogge. Wee came aboord, and told him what we had ſeene, and per-ſwaded him to ſtay a day or two in this place, telling him what refreſhing might there bee had : 10 but by no meanes would he ſtay, who was not pleaſed with the motion. So we left the Fowle, and loſt our way downe to the South-weſt, before they went in ſight of the Land, which now beares to the Eaſt from vs, being the ſame mayne Land that wee had all this while followed. Now, we had loſt the ſight of it, becauſe it falleth away to the Eaſt, after ſome fiue and twenty or thirty leagues. Now we came to the ſhallow water, wherewith wee were not acquainted ſince we came from *Iſland* ; now we came into broken ground and Rockes, through which we paſſed downe to the South. In this our courſe we had a ſtorme, and the water did ſhoald apace. Our Maſter came to an anchor in fifteene fathoms water.

Wee weighed and ſtood to the South-eaſt, becauſe the Land in this place did lie ſo. When we came to the point of the Weſt Land (for we now had Land on both ſides of vs) we came to 20 an anchor. Our Maſter ſent the Boat aſhoare, to ſee what that Land was, and whether there were any way through. They ſoone returned, and ſhewed that beyond the point of Land to the South, there was a large Sea. This Land on the Weſt ſide, was a very narrow Point. Wee weighed from hence, and ſtood in for this Sea betweene the two Lands, which (in this place) is not two leagues broad downe to the South, for a great way in ſight of the Eaſt ſhoare. In the end we loſt ſight thereof, and ſaw it not till we came to the bottome of the Bay, into ſixe or ſeuen fathomes water. Hence we ſtood vp to the North by the Weſt ſhoare, till wee came to an Iland in 53. where we tooke in water and ballaſt.

Diſcord : ſee From hence wee paſſed towards the North : but ſome two or three dayes after (reaſoning **Widhouſe his** concerning our comming into this Bay, and going out) our Maſter tooke occaſion to reuiue old 30 **Relations fol-** matters, and to diſplace *Robert Iuet* from being his Mate, and the Boat-ſwaine from his place, **lowing.** for words ſpoken in the firſt great Bay of Ice. Then hee made *Robert Billet* his Mate, and *Wil-* **Michaelmaſſe** *liam Wilſon* our Boat-ſwaine. Vp to the North wee ſtood, till we raiſed Land, then downe to **Day, and Bay.** the South, and vp to the North, then downe againe to the South : and on Michaelmaſſe day came in, and went out of certaine Lands : which our Maſter ſets downe by the name of *Michael-* *maſſe* Bay, becauſe we came in and went out on that day. From hence wee ſtood to the North, and came into ſhoald water ; and the weather being thicke and foule, wee came to an anchor in ſeuen or eight fathome water, and there lay eight dayes : in all which time wee could not get one houre to weigh our anchor. But the eight day, the wind beginning to ceaſe, our Maſter would haue the anchor vp, againſt the mind of all who knew what belonged thereunto. Well, 40 to it we went, and when we had brought it to a peake, a Sea tooke her, and caſt vs all off from **Anchor loſt.** the Capſtone, and hurt diuers of vs. Here wee loſt our Anchor, and if the Carpenter had not beene, we had loſt our Cable too : but he (fearing ſuch a matter) was ready with his Axe, and ſo cut it.

From hence we ſtood to the South, and to the South-weſt, through a cleere Sea of diuers **Sea of two co-** ſounding, and came to a Sea of two colours, one blacke, and the other white, ſixteene or ſeuen-**lours.** teene fathome water, betweene which we went foure or fiue leagues. But the night comming, we tooke in our Top-ſayles, and ſtood afore the wind with our Maine-ſayle and Fore-ſayle, and came into fiue or ſixe fathomes, and ſaw no Land for it was darke. Then we ſtood to the Eaſt, and had deepe water againe, then to the South and Southweſt, and ſo came to our Weſtermoſt 50 Bay of all, and came to an anchor neereſt to the North ſhoare. Out went our Boat to the Land that was next vs, when they came neere it, our Boat could not flote to the ſhoare it was **Footing of a** ſo ſhallow : yet aſhoare they got. Here our men ſaw the footing of a man and a Ducke in the **man.** ſnowy Rockes, and Wood good ſtore, whereof they tooke ſome and returned aboord. Being at anchor in this place, we ſaw a ledge of Rockes to the South of vs, ſome league of length ; It lay North and South, couered at a full Sea ; for a ſtrong tide ſetteth in here. At mid-night wee weighed, and ſtood to goe out as we came in ; and had not gone long, but the Carpenter came **Sticks on a** and told the Maſter, that if he kept that courſe he would be vpon the Rockes : the Maſter con-**Rocke.** ceiued that he was paſt them, when preſently wee ranne on them, and there ſtucke faſt twelue houres : but (by the mercy of God) we got off vnhurt, though not vnſcarred.   60

Wee ſtood vp to the Eaſt and rayſed three Hills, lying North and South : wee went to the furthermoſt, and left it to the North of vs, and ſo into a Bay, where wee came to an anchor. Here our Maſter ſent out our Boat, with my ſelfe and the Carpenter to ſeeke a place to winter in : and it was time ; for the nights were long and cold, and the earth couered with Snow. Ha-uing

uing spent three moneths in a Labyrinth without end, being now the last of October, we went downe to the East, to the bottome of the Bay : but returned without speeding of that we went for. The next day we went to the South, and the South-west, and found a place, whereunto we brought our ship, and haled her aground : and this was the first of Nouember. By the tenth thereof we were frozen in : but now we were in, it behooued vs to haue care of what we had; for, that we were sure of ; but what we had not, was vncertaine. *Last of Octo-ber.* *Nouember the tenth frozen in.*

Wee were victualled for sixe moneths in good proportion, and of that which was good : if our Master would haue had more, he might haue had it at home and in other places. Here we were now, and therefore it behoued vs so to spend, that wee might haue (when time came) to bring vs to the *Capes* where the Fowle bred, for that was all the hope wee had to bring vs home.
10 Wherefore our Master tooke order, first for the spending of that wee had, and then to increase it, by propounding a reward to them that killed either Beast, Fish, or Fowle, as in his Iournall you haue seene. About the middle of this moneth of Nouember, dyed *Iohn Williams* our Gunner. God pardon the Masters vncharitable dealing with this man. Now for that I am come to speake of him, out of whose ashes (as it were) that vnhappy deed grew which brought a scandall vpon all that are returned home, and vpon the action it selfe, the multitude (like the dog) running after the stone, but not at the caster : therefore, not to wrong the liuing, nor slander the dead, I will (by the leaue of God) deliuer the truth as neere as I can. *John Williams dyeth.*

You shall vnderstand, that our Master kept (in his house at *London*) a young man, named *Hen-rie Greene*, borne in *Kent*, of Worshipfull Parents, but by his lewd life and conuersation hee had
20 lost the good will of all his frinds, and had spent all that hee had. This man, our Master would haue to Sea with him, because hee could write well : our Master gaue him meate, and drinke, and lodging, and by meanes of one Master *Venson*, with much adoe got foure pounds of his mother to buy him clothes, wherewith Master *Venson* would not trust him : but saw it laid out himselfe. This *Henrie Greene* was not set downe in the owners booke, nor any wages made for him. Hee came first aboord at *Grauesend*, and at *Harwich* should haue gone into the field, with one *Wilkinson*. At *Island* the Surgeon and hee fell out in *Dutch*, and hee beat him a shoare in *English*, which set all the company in a rage ; so that wee had much adoe to get the Surgeon aboord. I told the Master of it, but hee bade mee let it alone, for (said hee) the Surgeon had a tongue that would wrong the best friend hee had. But *Robert Iuet* (the
30 Masters Mate) would needs burne his finger in the embers, and told the Carpenter a long tale (when hee was drunke) that our Master had brought in *Greene* to cracke his credit that should displease him : which words came to the Masters eares, who when hee vnderstood it, would haue gone backe to *Island*, when he was fortie leagues from thence, to haue sent home his Mate *Robert Iuet* in a Fisher-man. But, being otherwise perswaded, all was well. So *Henry Greene* stood vpright, and very inward with the Master, and was a seruiceable man euery way for manhood : but for Religion he would say, he was cleane paper whereon he might write what hee would. Now, when our Gunner was dead, and (as the order is in such cases) if the company stand in need of any thing that belonged to the man deceased, then is it brought to the Mayne
40 Mast, and there sold to them that will giue most for the same : This Gunner had a gray cloth gowne, which *Greene* prayed the Master to friend him so much as to let him haue it, paying for it as another would giue : the Master saith hee should, and thereupon hee answered some, that sought to haue it, that *Greene* should haue it, and none else, and so it rested. *Henry Greenes bad conditions*

Now out of season and time, the Master calleth the Carpenter to goe in hand with an house on shoare, which at the beginning our Master would not heare, when it might haue beene done. The Carpenter told him, that the Snow and Frost were such, as hee neither could, nor would goe in hand with such worke. Which when our Master heard, hee ferreted him out of his Cabbin to strike him, calling him by many foule names, and threatning to hang him. The Carpenter told him that hee knew what belonged to his place better then himselfe, and that hee was no
50 House Carpenter. So this passed, and the house was (after) made with much labour, but to no end. The next day after the Master and the Carpenter fell out, the Carpenter tooke his Peece and *Henry Greene* with him, for it was an order that none should goe out alone, but one with a Peece, and another with a Pike. This did moue the Master so much the more against *Henry Greene*, that *Robert Billet* his Mate must haue the gowne, and had it deliuered vnto him ; which when *Henry Greene* saw, he challenged the Masters promise : but the Master did so raile on *Greene*, with so many words of disgrace, telling him, that all his friends would not trust him with twenty shillings, and therefore why should he ? As for wages he had none, nor none should haue, if he did not please him well. Yet the Master had promised him to make his wages as good, as any mans in the ship; and to haue him one of the Princes guard when we came home. But you
60 shall see how the deuil out of this so wrought with *Green*, that he did the Master what mischiefe hee could in seeking to discredit him, and to thrust him and many other honest men out of the Ship in the end. To speake of all our trouble in this time of Winter (which was so cold, as it lamed the most of our Company, and my selfe doe yet feele it) would bee too tedious. *Greenes con-spiracie.* *Their hard wintring.*

But I must not forget to shew, how mercifully God dealt with vs in this time ; for the

space

Store of Partridges.

space of three moneths wee had such store of Fowle of one kinde (which were Partridges as white as milke) that wee killed aboue an hundred dozen, besides others of sundry sorts : for all was fish that came to the net. The Spring comming, this Fowle left vs, yet they were with vs all the extreame cold. Then in their places came diuers sort of other Fowle, as

Other Fowles succeeding in their seasons.

Swanne, Geese, Duck, and Teale, but hard to come by. Our Master hoped they would haue bred in those broken grounds, but they doe not : but came from the South, and flew to the North, further then we were this Voyage; yet if they be taken short with the wind at North, or North-west, or North-east, then they fall and stay till the winde serue them, and then flye to the North. Now in time these Fowles are gone, and few or none to bee seene. Then wee went into the Woods, Hilles, and Valleyes, for all things that had any shew of substance in them, how vile soeuer : the mosse of the ground, then the which I take the powder of

Miserable diet

a post to bee much better, and the Frogge (in his ingendring time as loathsome as a Toade) was not spared. But amongst the diuers sorts of buds, it pleased God that Thomas Woodhouse brought home a budde of a Tree, full of a Turpentine substance. Of this our

Medicinable budde.

Surgeon made a decoction to drinke, and applyed the buddes hot to them that were troubled with ach in any part of their bodies ; and for my part, I confesse, I receiued great and present ease of my paine.

A Sauage.

About this time, when the Ice began to breake out of the Bayes, there came a Sauage to our Ship, as it were to see and to bee seene, being the first that we had seene in all this time : whom our Master intreated well, and made much of him, promising vnto himselfe great matters by his meanes, and therefore would haue all the Kniues and Hatchets (which any man had) to his priuate vse, but receiued none but from Iohn King the Carpenter, and my selfe. To this Sauage our Master gaue a Knife, a Looking-glasse, and Buttons, who receiued them thankefully, and made signes that after hee had slept hee would come againe, which hee did. When hee came, hee brought with him a Sled, which hee drew after him, and

Turke.

vpon it two Deeres skinnes, and two Beauer skinnes. Hee had a scrip vnder his arme, out of which hee drew those things which the Master had giuen him. Hee tooke the Knife and laid it vpon one of the Beauer skinnes, and his Glasses and Buttons vpon the other, and so gaue them to the Master, who receiued them ; and the Sauage tooke those things which the Master had giuen him, and put them vp into his scrip againe. Then the Master shewed him an Hatchet, for which hee would haue giuen the Master one of his Deere skinnes, but our Master would haue them both, and so hee had, although not willingly. After many signes of people to the North, and to the South, and that after so many sleepes he would come againe, he went his way, but neuer came more.

Fishing.

Now the Ice being out of the Sounds, so that our Boat might go from one place vnto another, a company of men were appointed by the Master to goa fishing with our net ; their names were as followeth : William Wilson, Henry Greene, Michael Perce, Iohn Thomas, Andrew Moter, Bennet Mathewes, and Arnold Lodlo. These men, the first day they went, caught fiue hundred fish, as big as good Herrings, and some Troutes : which put vs all in some hope to haue our wants supplied, and our Commons amended : but these were the most that euer they got in one day, for many dayes they got not a quarter so many. In this time of their fishing, Henry Green and William Wilson, with some others, plotted to take the net and the shallop, which the Carpenter had now set vp, and so to shift for themselues. But the shallop being readie, our Master would goe in it himselfe, to the South and South-west, to see if hee could meete with the people ; for, to that end was it set vp, and (that way) wee might see the Woods set on fire by them. So the Master tooke the Sayue and the Shallop, and so much victuall as would serue for eight or nine dayes, and to the South hee went. They that remained aboord, were to take in water, wood, and ballast, and to haue all things in a readinesse against hee came backe. But hee set no time of his returne ; for hee was perswaded, if he could meet with the people, hee should haue flesh of them, and that good store : but hee returned worse then hee went forth. For, hee could by no meanes meete with the people, although they were neere them, yet they would set the woods on fire in his sight.

Being returned, hee fitted all things for his returne, and first, deliuered all the bread out of the bread roome (which came to a pound a piece for euery mans share) and deliuered also a Bill of Returne, willing them to haue that to shew, if it pleased God, that they came home: and he wept when hee gaue it vnto them. But to helpe vs in this poore estate with some reliefe, the Boate and Sayue went to worke on Friday morning, and stayed till Sunday noone : at which time they came aboord, and brought fourescore small Fish, a poore reliefe for so many hungry bellies. Then we wayed, and stood out of our wintering place, and came to an Anchor without, in the mouth of the Bay: from whence we wayed and came to an anchor without in the Sea, where our bread

Belly straits.

being gone, that store of cheese we had was to stop a gap, whereof there were fiue, whereat the company grudged, because they made account of nine. But those that were left, were equally diuided by the Master, although he had counsell to the contrarie: for there were some who hauing it, would make hast to bee rid thereof, because they could not gouerne it. I knew when Henrie

Greene

Greene gaue halfe his bread, which hee had for fourteene dayes, to one to keepe, and prayed him not to let him haue any vntill the next Munday : but before Wednesday at night, hee neuer left till hee had it againe, hauing eaten vp his first weekes bread before. So Wilson the Boat-swaine hath eaten (in one day) his fortnights bread, and hath beene two or three dayes sicke for his labour. The cause that moued the Master to deliuer all the Cheese, was because they were not all of one goodnesse, and therefore they should see that they had no wrong done them : but euery man should haue alike the best and the worst together, which was three pounds and a halfe for seuen dayes.

The wind seruing, we weighed and stood to the North-west, and on Munday at night (the
10 eighteenth day of Iune) wee fell into the Ice, and the next day the wind being at West, we lay there till Sunday in sight of Land. Now being here, the Master told Nicholas Simmes, that there would be a breaking vp of chests, and a search for bread, and willed him (if hee had any) to bring it to him, which hee did, and deliuered to the Master thirty cakes in a bagge. This deed of the Master (if it bee true) hath made mee maruell, what should bee the reason that hee did not stop the breach in the beginning, but let it grow to that height, as that it ouerthrew himselfe and ma-ny other honest men : but *there are many deuices in the heart of man, yet the counsell of the Lord shall stand.*

Being thus in the Ice on Saturday, the one and twentieth of Iune at night, Wilson the ~~Wilson & Green,~~
Boatswayne, and Henry Greene came to mee lying (in my Cabbin) lame, and told mee that they ~~their wicked-~~
20 and the rest of their Associates, would shift the Company, and turne the Master, and all the sicke ~~nesse.~~
men into the shallop, & let them shift for themselues. For, there was not fourteene daies victuall left for all the Company, at that poore allowance they were at, and that there they lay, the Master not caring to goe one way or other : and that they had not eaten any thing these three dayes, and therefore were resolute, either to mend or end, and what they had begun they would goe through with it, or dye. When I heard this, I told them I maruelled to heare so much from them, considering that they were married men, and had wiues and children, and that for their sakes they should not commit so foule a thing in the sight of God and man, as that would bee ; for why should they banish themselues from their natiue Countrie ? Henry Greene bad me hold my peace, for he knew the worst, which was, to be hanged when hee came home, and therefore of the two
30 he would rather be hanged at home then starued abroad : and for the good will they bare me, they would haue mee stay in the Ship. I gaue them thankes, and told them that I came into her, not to forsake her, yet not to hurt my selfe and others by any such deed. Henry Greene told me then, that I must take my fortune in the Shallop. If there bee no remedie (said I) the will of God bee done.

Away went Henry Greene in a rage, swearing to cut his throat that went about to disturbe them, and left Wilson by me, with whom I had some talke, but to no good : for he was so persua-ded, that there was no remedie now, but to goe on while it was hot, least their partie should faile them, and the mischiefe they had intended to others should light on themselues. Henry Greene came againe, and demanded of him what I said. Wilson answered, He is in his old song, still pati-
40 ent. Then I spake to Henry Greene to stay three dayes, in which time I would so deale with the Master, that all should be well. So I dealt with him to forbeare but two dayes, nay twelue houres; there is no way then (say they) but out of hand. Then I told them, that if they would stay till Munday, I would ioyne with them to share all the victuals in the ship, and would iustifie it when I came home; but this would not serue their turnes. Wherefore I told them, it was some worse matter they had in hand then they made shew of, and that it was bloud and reuenge hee sought, or else he would not at such a time of night vndertake such a deed. Henry Greene (with that) ta-keth my Bible which lay before me, and sware that hee would doe no man harme, and what hee did was for the good of the voyage, and for nothing else ; and that all the rest should do the like. The like did Wilson sweare.

50 Henry Greene went his way, and presently came Iuet, who because hee was an ancient man, ~~Robert Iuet. See~~
I hoped to haue found some reason in him ; but hee was worse then Henry Greene, for hee sware ~~Withouses~~
plainely that he would iustifie this deed when he came home. After him came Iohn Thomas, and ~~notes.~~
Michel Perce, as birds of one feather : but because they are not liuing I will let them goe, as then I did. Then came Moter and Bennet, of whom I demanded, if they were well aduised what they had taken in hand. They answered, they were, and therefore came to take their oath.

Now, because I am much condemned for this oath, as one of them that plotted with them, and that by an oath I should bind them together to performe what they had begun, I thought good heere to set downe to the view of all, how well their oath and deedes agreed : and thus it was. *You shall sweare truth to God, your Prince and Countrie : you shall doe nothing, but to the glory of* ~~Oath abused.~~
60 *God, and the good of the action in hand, and harme to no man.* This was the oath, without ad-ding or diminishing. I looked for more of these companions (although these were too many) but there came no more. It was darke, and they in a readinesse to put this deed of darknesse in exe-cution. I called to Henry Greene and Wilson, and prayed them not to goe in hand with it in the darke, but to stay till the morning. Now, euerie man (I hope) would goe to his rest, but wic-

kednesse

kednéſſe ſleepeth not ; for *Henry Greene* keepeth the Maſter company all night (and gaue mee bread,which his Cabbin-mate gaue him) and others are as watchfull as he. Then I asked *Henrie Greene*, whom he would put out with the Maſter ? he ſaid, the Carpenter *Iohn King*, and the ſicke men. I ſaid, they ſhould not doe well to part with the Carpenter , what need ſoeuer they ſhould haue. Why the Carpenter was in no more regard amongſt them, was ; firſt, for that he and *Iohn King* were condemned for wrong done in the victuall. But the chiefeſt cauſe was , for that the Maſter loued him, and made him his Mate, vpon his returne out of our wintering place, thereby diſplacing *Robert Billet* , whereat they did grudge , becauſe hee could neither write nor read. And therefore (ſaid they) the Maſter and his ignorant Mate would carry the Ship whither the Maſter pleaſed : the Maſter forbidding any man to keepe account or reckoning, hauing taken from all men whatſoeuer ſerued for that purpoſe. Well, I obtained of *Henrie Greene* and *Wilſon,* 10 **The Carpenter ſpared.** that the Carpenter ſhould ſtay, by whoſe meanes I hoped (after they had ſatisfied themſelues) that the Maſter, and the poore man might be taken into the Ship againe. Or, I hoped,that ſome one or other would giue ſome notice, either to the Carpenter *Iohn King*, or the Maſter ; for ſo it might haue come to paſſe by ſome of them that were the moſt forward.

Now, it ſhall not bee amiſſe to ſhew how we were lodged, and to begin in the Cooke roome ; there lay *Bennet* and the Cooper lame ; without the Cooke roome, on the ſteere-board ſide, lay *Thomas Wydhouſe* ſicke ; next to him lay *Sydrack Faner* lame, then the Surgeon, and *Iohn Hudſon* with him ; next to them lay *Wilſon* the Boatſwaine, and then *Arnold Lodlo* next to him : in the Gun-roome lay *Robert Iuet* and *Iohn Thomas* ; on the Lar-boord ſide , lay *Michael Bute* and *A-*20 *dria Moore* , who had neuer beene well ſince wee loſt our Anchor ; next to them lay *Michael Perce* and *Andrew Moter.* Next to them without the Gun-roome, lay *Iohn King*, and with him *Robert Billet :* next to them my ſelfe,and next to me *Francis Clements :* In the mid-ſhip,betweene the Capſtone and the Pumpes , lay *Henrie Greene* and *Nicholas Simmes.* This night *Iohn King* was late vp,and they thought he had been with the Maſter,but he was with the Carpenter,who lay on the Poope ; and comming downe from him, was met by his Cabbin-mate , as it were by chance,and ſo they came to their Cabbin together. It was not long ere it was day : the came *Bennet* for water for the Kettle, hee roſe and went into the Hold : when hee was in,they ſhut the Hatch on him (but who kept it downe I know not) vp vpon the Deck went *Bennet*.

In the meane time *Henrie Greene*, and another went to the Carpenter, and held him with a 30 **They bind the Maſter.** talke, till the Maſter came out of his Cabbin (which hee ſoone did) then came *Iohn Thomas* and *Bennet* before him, while *Wilſon* bound his armes behind him. He asked them what they meant ? they told him, he ſhould know when he was in the Shallop. Now *Iuet*, while this was a doing, came to *Iohn King* into the Hold, who was prouided for him, for he had got a ſword of his own, and kept him at a bay, and might haue killed him, but others came to helpe him : and ſo he came vp to the Maſter. The Maſter called to the Carpenter, and told him that he was bound ; but, I heard no anſwere he made. Now *Arnold Lodlo*,and *Michael Bute* rayled at them, and told them their knauerie would ſhew it ſelfe. Then was the Shallop haled vp to the Ship ſide , and the poore , ſicke , and lame men were called vpon to get them out of their Cabbins into the Shallop. The Maſter called to me, who came out of my Cabbin as well as I could, to the Hatch 40 way to ſpeake with him : where, on my knees I beſought them, for the loue of God, to remem-ber themſelues,and to doe as they would be done vnto. They bad me keepe my ſelfe well, and get me into my Cabbin ; not ſuffering the Maſter to ſpeake with me. But when I came into my Cabbin againe, hee called to me at the Horne, which gaue light into my Cabbin, and told mee that *Iuet* would ouerthrow vs all ; nay (ſaid I) it is that villaine *Henrie Greene*, and I ſpake it not ſoftly.

Now was the Carpenter at libertie, who asked them, if they would bee hanged when they came home : and as for himſelfe, hee ſaid, hee would not ſtay in the Ship vnleſſe they **The Carpenter let goe.** would force him : they bad him goe then, for they would not ſtay him : I will (ſaid hee) ſo I may haue my cheſt with mee, and all that is in it : they ſaid, hee ſhould, and preſently they 50 put it into the Shallop. Then hee came downe to mee, to take his leaue of mee, who perſwaded him to ſtay, which if he did , he might ſo worke that all ſhould bee well : hee ſaid, hee did not thinke, but they would be glad to take them in againe. For he was ſo perſwaded by the Ma-ſter, that there was not one in all the ſhip , that could tell how to carrie her home ; but (ſaith he) if we muſt part (which wee will not willingly doe , for they would follow the ſhip) hee prayed me , if wee came to the Capes before them, that I would leaue ſome token that wee had beene there, neere to the place where the Fowles bred, and hee would doe the like for vs : and ſo (with teares) we parted. Now were the ſicke men driuen out of their Cabbins into the Shallop ; but *Iohn Thomas* was *Francis Clements* friend, and *Bennet* was the Coopers, ſo as there were words betweene them and *Henrie Greene*, one ſaying,that they ſhould goe, and the other ſwea- 60 ring that they ſhould not goe , but ſuch as were in the ſhallop ſhould returne. When *Henrie Greene* heard that, he was compelled to giue place, and to put out *Arnold Lodlo*, and *Michael Bute*, which with much adoe they did.

In the meane time, there were ſome of them that plyed their worke, as if the Ship had beene
entred

entred by force, and they had free leaue to pillage, breaking vp Chefts, and rifling all places. One of them came by me, who asked me, what they fhould doe. I anfwered, hee fhould make an end of what hee had begun ; for I faw him doe nothing but fharke vp and downe. Now, were all the poore men in the Shallop, whofe names are as followeth; *Henrie Hudfon, Iohn Hudfon, Arnold Ledlo, Sidrack Faner, Phillip Staffe, Thomas Woodhoufe,* or *Wydhoufe, Adam Moore, Henrie King, Michael Bute.* The Carpenter got of them a Peece, and Powder, and Shot, and fome Pikes, an Iron Pot, with fome meale, and other things. They ftood out of the Ice, the Shallop being faft to the Sterne of the Shippe, and fo (when they were nigh out, for I cannot fay, they were cleane out) they cut her head faft from the Sterne of our Ship, then out with their Top-fayles, and towards the Eaft they ftood in a cleere Sea. In the end they tooke in their Top-fayles,
10 righted their Helme, and lay vnder their Fore-fayle till they had ranfacked and fearched all places in the Ship. In the Hold they found one of the veffels of meale whole, and the other halfe fpent, for wee had but two; wee found alfo two firkins of Butter, fome twentie feuen piece of Porke, halfe a bufhell of Peafe, but in the Mafters Cabbin we found two hundred of bisket Cakes, a pecke of Meale, of Beere to the quantitie of a Butt, one with another. Now, it was faid, that the Shallop was come within fight, they let fall the Main-fayle, and out with their Top-fayles, and flye as from an Enemy.

Then I prayed them yet to remember themfelues : but *William Wilfon* (more then the reft) would heare of no fuch matter. Comming nigh the Eaft fhoare they caft about, and ftood to the Weft and came to an Iland, and anchored in fixteene or feuenteene fathome water. So they fent
20 the Boat, and the Net afhoare to fee if they could haue a Draught : but could not for Rocks and great ftones. *Michael Perfe* killed two Fowle, and heere they found good ftore of that Weede, which we called Cockle-graffe in our wintering place, whereof they gathered ftore, and came aboard againe. Heere we lay that night, and the beft part of the next day, in all which time we faw not the fhallop, or euer after. Now *Henrie Greene* came to me and told mee, that it was the Companies will, that I fhould come vp into the Mafters Cabbin, and take charge thereof. I told him it was more fit for *Robert Iuet :* he faid, he fhould not come in it, nor meddle with the Mafters Card, or Iournals. So vp I came, and *Henrie Greene* gaue me the Key of the Mafters Cheft, and told me then, that he had laid the Mafters beft things together, which hee would vfe himfelfe when time did ferue : the bread was alfo deliuered me by tale.

30 The wind feruing, we ftood to the North-eaft, and this was *Robert Billets* courfe, contrarie to *Robert Iuet,* who would haue gone to the North-weft. We had the Eafterne fhoare ftill in fight, and (in the night) had a ftout gale of wind, and ftood afore it, till wee met with Ice, into the which we ranne from thinne to thicke, till we could goe no further for Ice, which lay fo thicke ahead of vs (and the wind brought it after vs afterne) that wee could not ftirre backward, nor forward : but fo lay imbayed fourteene daies in worfe Ice, then euer wee met to deale withall, for we had beene where there was greater ftore, but it was not fo broad vpon the water as this : for this floting Ice contained miles, and halfe miles in compaffe, where we had a deepe Sea, and a Tide of flood and ebbe, which fet North-weft and South-eaft. Heere *Robert Iuet* would haue gone to the North-weft, but *Robert Billet* was confident to go through to the North-eaft, which
40 he did. At laft, being cleere of this Ice, he continued his courfe in fight of the Eafterne fhoare, till he raifed foure Ilands which lay North and South : but we paffed them fixe or feuen leagues, the wind tooke vs fo fhort. Then wee ftood backe to them againe, and came to an Anchor betweene two of the moft Northermoft. We fent the Boat afhoare, to fee if there were any thing there to be had, but found nothing, but cockle Graffe, whereof they gathered ftore, and fo returned aboard. Before we came to this place, I might well fee, that I was kept in the fhip againft *Henry Greenes* minde, becaufe I did not fauour their proceedings better then I did. Then hee began (very fubtilly) to draw me to take vpon me to fearch for thofe things, which himfelfe had ftolne : and accufed me of a matter no leffe then Treafon amongft vs, that I had deceiued the
50 company of thirtie Cakes of bread. Now they began to talke amongft themfelues, that *England* was no fafe place for them, and *Henry Greene* fwore, the fhippe fhould not come into any place (but keepe the Sea ftill) till he had the Kings Majefties hand and Seale to fhew for his fafetie. They had many deuices in their heads, but *Henry Greene* in the end was their Captaine, and fo called of them.

From thefe Ilands we ftood to the North-eaft and the Eafter Land ftill in fight : wee rayfed thofe Ilands, that our Mafter called *Rumnies* Ilands. Betweene thefe Ilands and the fhallow ground to the Eaft of them, our Mafter went downe into the firft great Bay. We kept the Eaft fhoare ftill in our fight, and comming thwart of the low Land, wee ranne on a Rocke that lay vnder water, and ftrooke but once; for if fhee had, we might haue beene made Inhabitans of that
60 place : but God fent vs foone off without any harme that wee faw. Wee continued our courfe and rayfed Land a head of vs, which ftretched out to the North : which when they faw, they faid plainly, that *Robert Billet* by his Northerly courfe had left the Capes to the South, and that they were beft to feeke downe to the South in time for reliefe, before all was gone : for we had fmall ftore left. But *Robert Billet* would follow the Land to the North, faying, that he hoped in

Marginal notes:
The names of the company expofed in the Shallop,

Laft fight of the Shallop.

Foure Ilands.

The wicked flee where none purfueth

God

God to find ſomewhat to releeue vs that way, as ſoone as to the South. I told them that this Land was the Mayne of *Worſenhome* Cape, and that the ſhallow rockie ground, was the ſame that the Maſter went downe by, when he went into the great Bay. *Robert Iuet* and all ſaid, it was not poſſible, vnleſſe the Maſter had brought the ſhip ouer Land, and willed them to looke into the Maſters Card, and their courſe how well they did agree. We ſtood to the Eaſt, and left the mayne Land to the North, by many ſmall Ilands into a narrow gut betweene two Lands, and there came to an Anchor. The Boat went aſhoare on the North ſide, where wee found the great *Horne,* but nothing elſe. The next day wee went to the South ſide, but found nothing

Cockle graſſe. there, ſaue Cockle graſſe of which we gathered. This graſſe was a great releefe vnto vs, for with-out it, we ſhould hardly haue got to the Capes for want of victuall. The wind ſeruing we ſtood out, but before we could get cleane out, the wind came to the Weſt, ſo that we were conſtray-ned to anchor on the North ſide. [10]

The next day, wee weighed and doubled the point of the North Land, which is high Land, and ſo continueth to the Capes, lying North and South, ſome fiue and twentie or thirtie leagues. To the North we ſtood to ſee ſtore of thoſe Fowles that breed in the Capes, and to kill ſome with our ſhot, and to fetch them with our Boat. We raiſed the Capes with joy, and bare for them, and came to the Ilands that lie in the mouth of the ſtreight : but bearing in betweene

A Rocke. the Rockie Iles, we ranne on a Rocke that lay vnder water, and there ſtucke faſt eight or nine houres. It was ebbing water when we thus came on, ſo the floud ſet vs afloat, God guiding both wind and Sea, that it was calme, and faire weather : the ebbe came from the Eaſt, and the floud

Note. from the Weſt. When wee were afloat, wee ſtood more neere to the Eaſt ſhoare, and there [20] anchored.

Iuly 27. The next day being the ſeuen and twentieth of Iuly, we ſent the Boat to fetch ſome Fowle, and the ſhip ſhould way and ſtand as neere as they could : for the wind was againſt vs. They had a great way to row, and by that meanes they could not reach to the place where the Fowle bred : but found good ſtore of *Gulls,* yet hard to come by, on the Rocks and Clifes, but with their Peeces they killed ſome thirtie, and towards night returned. Now we had brought our ſhip more neere to the mouth of the Streights, and there came to an anchor in eighteen or twentie fathom water, vpon a Riffe or ſhelfe of ground : which after they had weighed their Anchor, and ſtood more neere to the place where the Fowle bred, they could not find it againe, nor no place like it : but were faine to turne to and fro in the mouth of the Streight, and to be in danger of Rockes, [30] becauſe they could not find ground to let fall an Anchor in, the water was ſo deepe.

Sauages. The eight and twentieth day, the Boat went to *Digges* his Cape for Fowle, and made direct-ly for the place where the Fowle bred, and being neere, they ſaw ſeuen Boates come about the Eaſterne point towards them. When the Sauages ſaw our Boate, they drew themſelues toge-ther, and drew their leſſer Boats into their bigger : and when they had done, they came rowing to our Boat, and made ſignes to the Weſt, but they made readie for all aſſayes. The Sauages came to them, and by ſignes grew familiar one with another, ſo as our men tooke one of theirs into our Boate, and they tooke one of ours into their Boate. Then they carried our man to a Coue where their Tents ſtood toward the Weſt of the place, where the Fowle bred : ſo they carried him into their Tents, where he remayned till our men returned with theirs. Our Boat went to [40] the place where the Fowle bred, and were deſirous to know how the Sauages killed their Fowle :

Sauages man-ner of fowling. he ſhewed them the manner how, which was thus, They take a long Pole with a ſnare at the end, which they put about the Fowles necke, and ſo plucke them downe. When our men knew that they had a better way of their owne, they ſhewed him the vſe of our Peeces, which at one ſhot would kill ſeuen or eight. To be ſhort, our Boat returned to their Coue for our man, and to deliuer theirs. When they came they made great joy, with dancing and leaping, and ſtroking of their breſts : they offered diuers things to our men, but they only tooke ſome Morſes Teeth, which they gaue them for a Knife, and two glaſſe buttons : and ſo receiuing our man they came aboard, much rejoycing at this chance, as if they had met with the moſt ſimple and kind people of the World. [50]

Greenes confi-dence. And *Henry Greene* (more then the reſt) was ſo confident, that (by no meanes) we ſhould take care to ſtand vpon our Guard : God blinding him ſo, that where hee made reckoning to receiue great matters from theſe people, he receiued more then he looked for, and that ſuddenly by being made a good example for all men : that make no conſcience of doing euill, and that we take heed of the Sauage people, how ſimple ſoeuer they ſeeme to be.

The next day, the nine and twentieth of Iuly, they made haſte to be aſhoare, and becauſe the ſhip rid too farre off, they weighed and ſtood as neere to the place where the Fowle bred, as they could : and becauſe I was lame, I was to goe in the Boat, to carrie ſuch things, as I had in the Cabbin of euery thing ſomewhat : and ſo with more haſte then good ſpeed (and not without ſwearing) away we went, *Henry Greene, William Wilſon, Iohn Thomas, Michael Perſe, Andrew* [60] *Moter,* and my ſelfe. When we came neere the ſhoare, the people were on the Hils, dancing and leaping : to the Coue we came, where they had drawne vp their Boates : wee brought our Boate to the Eaſt ſide of the Coue, cloſe to the Rockes. Aſhoare they went, and made faſt the

Boat

Boat to a great stone on the shoare, the people came, and euery one had somewhat in his hand to barter : but *Henry Greene* swore they should haue nothing, till he had Venison, for that they had so promised him by signes.

Now when we came, they made signes to their Dogges (whereof there were many like Mongrels, as bigge as Hounds) and pointed to their Mountaine, and to the Sunne, clapping their hands. Then *Henry Greene, Iohn Thomas*, and *William Wilson*, stood hard by the Boate head, *Michael Perse*, and *Andrew Moter* were got vp vpon the Rocke, a gathering of Sorrell : not one of them had any weapon about him, not so much as a sticke, saue *Henry Greene* only, who had a piece of a Pike in his hand : nor saw I any thing that they had wherewith to hurt vs. *Henry Greene* and *William Wilson* had Looking-glasses, and Iewes Trumps, and Bels, which they were shewing the people. The Sauages standing round about them, one of them came into the Boats head to me to shew me a Bottle : I made signes to him to get him ashoare, but he made as though he had not vnderstood me, whereupon I stood vp, and pointed him ashoare. In the meane-time, another stole behind me to the sterne of the Boat, and when I saw him athoare, that was in the head of the Boat, I sate downe againe : but suddenly I saw the legge and foote of a man by mee. Wherefore I cast vp my head, and saw the Sauage with his Knife in his hand, who strooke at my brest ouer my head : I cast vp my right arme to saue my brest, he wounded my arme, and strooke me into the bodie vnder my right Pappe. He strooke a second blow which I met with my left hand, and then he strooke me into the right thigh, and had like to haue cut off my little finger of the left hand. Now, I had got hold of the string of the Knife, and had woond it about my left hand, he striuing with both his hands, to make an end of that he had begunne, I found him but weake in the gripe (God enabling me) and getting hold of the sleeue of his left arme, so bare him from me. His left side lay bare to me, which when I saw, I put his sleeue off his left arme into my left hand, holding the string of the Knife fast in the same hand: and hauing got my right hand at libertie, I sought for somewhat wherewith to strike him (not remembring my Dagger at my side) but looking downe I saw it, and therewith strooke him into the bodie, and the throate.

Whiles I was thus assaulted in the Boat, our men were set vpon on the shoare. *Iohn Thomas* and *William Wilson* had their bowels cut, and *Michael Perse* and *Henry Greene* being mortally wounded, came tumbling into the Boat together. When *Andrew Moter* saw this medley, hee came running downe the Rockes, and leaped into the Sea, and so swamme to the Boat, hanging on the sterne thereof, till *Michael Perse* tooke him in, who manfully made good the head of the Boat against the Sauages, that pressed sore vpon vs. Now *Michael Perse* had got an Hatchet, wherewith I saw him strike one of them, that he lay sprawling in the Sea. *Henry Greene* crieth *Coragio*, and layeth about him with his Truncheon : I cryed to them to cleere the Boat, and *Andrew Moter* cryed to bee taken in : the Sauages betooke them to their Bowes and Arrowes, which they sent amongst vs, wherewith *Henry Greene* was slaine out-right, and *Michael Perse* receiued may wounds, and so did the rest. *Michael Perse* cleereth the Boate, and puts it from the shoare, and helpeth *Andrew Moter* in : but in turning of the Boat, I receiued a cruell wound in my backe with an Arrow. *Michael Perse* and *Andrew Moter* rowed the Boate away, which when the Sauages saw, they ranne to their Boats, and I feared they would haue launched them, to haue followed vs, but they did not, and our ship was in the middle of the channell, and could not see vs.

Now, when they had rowed a good way from the shoare, *Michael Perse* fainted, and could row no more : then was *Andrew Moter* driuen to stand in the Boat head, and waft to the ship, which (at the first) saw vs not, and when they did, they could not tel what to make of vs, but in the end they stood for vs, and so tooke vs vp. *Henry Greene* was throwne out of the Boat into the Sea, and the rest were had aboard, the Sauage being yet aliue, yet without sense. But they died all there that day, *William Wilson* swearing and cursing in most fearefull manner : *Michael Perse* liued two dayes after, and then died. Thus you haue heard the Tragicall end of *Henry Greene* and his Mates, whom they called Captaine, these foure being the only lustie men in all the ship.

The poore number that was left, were to ply our ship to and fro, in the mouth of the streight, for there was no place to anchor in neere hand : besides, they were to goe in the Boate to kill Fowle, to bring vs home, which they did, although with danger to vs all. For if the wind blew, there was an high Sea, and the eddies of the Tydes would carrie the ship so neere the Rockes, as it feared our Master, for so I will now call him. After they had killed some two hundred Fowle, with great labour on the South Cape, wee stood to the East : but when wee were fixe or seuen leagues from the Capes, the wind came vp at East. Then wee stood backe to the Capes againe, and killed an hundred Fowle more. After this, the wind came to the West, so wee were driuen to goe away, and then our Master stood (for the most) along by the North shoare, till he fell into broken ground about the *Queenes Fore-land*, and there anchored. From thence wee went to *Gods Mercies*, and from thence to those Ilands, which lye in the mouth of our Streight, not seeing the Land, till we were readie to runne our Bosprite against the Rockes in a fogge. But it cleered a little, and then we might see our selues inclosed with Rockie Ilands, and could find no

ground

(marginal notes)
Sauages dogges.
Sauages trecherie.
Trecherie iust to vniust Tray-tors.
Greene slaine.
Wicked and wretched end of wretched wicked men.

ground to anchor in. There our Master lay atrie all night, and the next day the fogge continuing, they sought for ground to anchor in, and found some in an hundred and odde fathomes of water. The next day we weighed and stood to the East, but before wee came heere, we had put our selues to hard allowance, as halfe a foule a day with the pottage : for yet we had some meale left, and nothing else. Then they beganne to make triall of all whatsoeuer : wee had flayed our **Miserie pursueth the rest.** Fowle, for they wil not pull : and *Robert Iuet* was the first, that made vse of the skins by burning of the Feathers : so they became a great dish of meate , and as for the garbidge, it was not throwne away.

After we were cleere of these Ilands, which lie out with two points, one to the South-east, and the other to the North, making a Bay to the sight as if there were no way through, we continued our course East South-east, and South and by East, to raise *the Desolations,* from thence to shape our course for *Ireland.* Thus we continued diuers dayes : but the wind comming against vs, made vs to alter our course, and by the meanes of *Robert Iuet* who perswaded the company, that they should find great reliefe in *Newfound Land* , if our Country-men were there, and if they were gone before we came, yet should we find great store of bread and fish left ashoare by them : but how true, I giue God thankes, we did not trie. Yet we stood to the South-west, and to the West, almost to fiftie seuen degrees : when (by the will of God) the winde came vp at Southwest. Then the Master asked me, if he should take the benefit of this wind, and shape his course for *Ireland.* I said it was best to goe, where we knew Corne grew, and not to seeke it, where it was cast away, and not to be found. Towards *Ireland* now wee stood, with prosperous winds for many dayes together : then was all our Meale spent, and our Fowle restie and dry : but (being no remedie) we were content with the Salt broth for Dinner, and the halfe Fowle for Supper. **Poore Diet.** Now went our Candles to wracke, and *Bennet* our Cooke made a messe of meate of the bones of the Fowle, frying them with Candle-grease, till they were crispe , and with Vineger put to them, made a good dish of meate. Our Vineger was shared, and to euery man a pound of Candles deliuered for a weeke, as a great daintie. Now *Robert Iuet* (by his reckoning) saith, wee were within sixtie or seuentie leagues of *Ireland,* when wee had two hundred thither. And sure our course was so much the longer, through our euill steeredge : for, our men became so weake, that they could not stand at the Helme, but were faine to sit.

Robert Iuets death. Then *Robert Iuet* dyed, for meere want, and all our men were in despaire, and said wee were past *Ireland,* and our last Fowle were in the steep-tub. So, our men cared not which end went forward, insomuch as our Master was driuen to looke to their labour, as well as his owne : for some of them would sit and see the fore-sayle , or mayne-sayle flie vp to the tops, the sheetes being either flowne or broken, and would not helpe it themselues, nor call to others for helpe, which much grieued the Master. Now in this extremitie it pleased God to giue vs sight of Land, not farre from the place our Master said he would fall withal, which was the Bay of *Galloway,* and we fell to the West of the *Derses,* and so stood along by the coast, to the South-west. In the end, there was a joyful cry, a sayle, a sayle, towards which they stood, then they saw more, but to the neerest **A sayle of *Fowy Bere* Hauen in *Ireland.*** we stood, and called to him : his Barke was of *Fowy,* and was at anchor a Fishing : he came to vs, and brought vs into *Bere* Hauen. Here we stayed a few dayes, and delt with the *Irish,* to supply our wants, but found no reliefe : for in this place there was neither Bread, Drinke, nor mony to be had amongst them. Wherfore they aduised vs to deale with our Country-men, who were there a fishing, which we did : but found them so cold in kindnesse, that they would doe nothing without present money, whereof we had none in the Ship. In the end, we procured one *Iohn Waymouth,* Master of the Barke that brought vs into this Harbour, to furnish vs with money, which hee did, and receiued our best Cable and Anchor in pawne for the same. With this money, our Master with the helpe of *Iohn Waymouth,* bought Bread, Beere, and Beefe.

Now, as wee were beholding to *Waymouth* for his money, so were wee to one Captaine *Taylor,* for making of our contracts with *Waymouth,* by whose meanes hee tooke a Bill for our Cable and Anchor, and for the mens Wages, who would not goe with vs, vnlesse *Waymouth* wold passe his word for the same : for they made shew, that they were not willing to goe with vs for any wages. Whereupon Captaine *Taylor* swore hee would presse them, and then, if they would not goe, hee would hang them.

In conclusion, wee agreed for three pound ten shillings a man, to bring our Ship to *Plimouth,* or *Dartmouth,* and to giue the Pilot fiue pound : but if the winde did not serue, but that they were driuen to put into *Bristow,* they were to haue foure pound ten shillings a man, and the Pilot sixe pound. Omitting therefore further circumstances, from *Bere* Hauen wee came to *Plimouth,* and so to an anchor, before the Castle : and from *Plimouth,* with faire winde and weather **They arriue at *Plimouth.*** without stop or stay, wee came to the *Downes,* from thence to *Grauesend,* where most of our men went a shoare, and from thence came on this side *Erith,* and there stopped : where our Master *Robert Billet* came aboord, and so had mee vp to *London* with him, and so wee came to Sir *Thomas Smiths* together.

Forasmuch as this report of Pricket *may happely bee suspected by some, as not so friendly to* Hudson, *who returned with that Companie which had so cruelly exposed* Hudson *and his, and therefore may seeme to lay heauier imputation, and rip vp occasions further then they will beleeue; I haue also added the report of* Thomas Widhoule, *one of the exposed Companie, who ascribeth those occasions of discord to* Iuet. *I take not on mee to sentence, no not to examine; I haue presented the Euidence iust as I had it: let the Bench censure, hearing with both eares, that which with both eyes they may see in those, and these notes; to which, I haue first prefixed his Letter to* Master Samuel Macham.

MAster Macham, *I heartily commend mee vnto you, &c. I can write vnto you no newes, though I haue seene much, but such as euery* English *Fisherman haunting these Coasts can report better*
10 *then my selfe.*

Wee kept our Whitsunday in the North-east end of Island; *and I thinke I neuer fared better in England then wee feasted there. They of the Countrey are very poore, and liue miserably: yet we found there-* Ilanders
in store of fresh Fish and daintie Fowle. I my selfe in an after-noone killed so much Fowle, as feasted all poore.
our Companie, being three and twentie persons at one time, onely with Partridges; besides Curlue, Plouer, Mallard, Teale, and Goose. I haue seene two hot Bathes in Island, *and haue beene in one of them. Wee are resolued to trie the vttermost, and lye onely expecting a faire winde, and to refresh our selues to auoyd the Ice, which now is come off the West Coasts, of which wee haue seene whole Ilands, but God bee* The cause of
thanked, haue not beene in danger of any. Thus I desire all your prayers for vs. From Island *this thir-* their stay at
tieth of May, 1610. Island.
20

A note found in the Deske of *Thomas Wydowse,* Student in the Mathematickes, hee being one of them who was put into the Shallop.

THe tenth day of September, 1610. after dinner, our Master called all the Companie together, to heare and beare witnesse of the abuse of some of the Companie (it hauing beene the request of Robert Iuet) that the Master should redresse some abuses and slanders, as hee called them, against this I-
30 uet: which thing after the Master had examined and heard with equitie what hee could say for himselfe, there were prooued so many and great abuses, and mutinous matters against the Master, and action by Iuet, that there was danger to haue suffred them longer: and it was fit time to punish and cut off farther occasions of the like mutinies.

It was prooued to his face, first with Bennet Mathew *our Trumpet vpon our first sight of* Island, and hee confest, that hee supposed that in the action would bee man-slaughter, and proue bloodie to some.

Secondly, at our comming from Island, in hearing of the companie, hee did threaten to turne the head of the Ship home from the action, which at that time was by our Master wisely pacified, hoping of amendment.

Thirdly, it was deposed by Philip Staffe *our Carpenter, and* Ladlie Arnold, *to his face vpon the holy*
40 *Bible, that hee perswaded them to keepe Muskets charged, and Swords readie in their Cabbins, for they should bee charged with shot, ere the Voyage were ouer.*

Fourthly, wee being pestered in the Ice, hee had vsed words tending to mutinie, discouragement, and slander of the action, which easily tooke effect in those that were timorous; and had not the Master in time preuented, it might easily haue ouerthrowne the Voyage: and now lately beeing imbayed in a deepe Bay, which the Master had desire to see, for some reasons to himselfe knowne, his word tended altogether to put the Companie into a fray of extremitie, by wintering in cold: Iesting at our Masters hope to see Bantam *by* Candlemasse.

For these and diuers other base slanders against the Master, hee was deposed; and Robert Bylot, *who had shewed himselfe honestly respecting the good of the action, was placed in his stead the Masters Mate.*

Also Francis Clement *the Boatson, at this time was put from his Office, and* William Wilson, *a*
50 *man thought more fit, preferred to his place. This man had basely carryed himselfe to our Master and to the action.*

Also Adrian Mooter *was appointed Boatsons mate: and a promise by the Master, that from this day Iuats wages should remaine to* Bylot, *and the Boatsons ouerplus of wages should bee equally diuided betweene* Wilson *and one* Iohn King, *to the owners good liking, one of the Quarter Masters, who had very well carryed themselues to the furtherance of the businesse.*

Also the Master promised, if the Offenders yet behaued themselues henceforth honestly, hee would bee a meanes for their good, and that hee would forget iniuries, with other admonitions.

These things thus premised touching Hudsons *exposing, and Gods iust iudgements on the Ex-*
60 *posers, as* Pricket *hath related (whom they reserued as is thought, in hope by* Sir Dudley Digges *his Master to procure their pardon at their returne) I thought good to adde that which I haue further receiued from good Intelligence, that the Ship comming aground at* Digges *Iland, in* 62. *degrees* 44. *minutes, a great flood came from the West and set them on floate: an argument of an open passage from the South Sea to that, and consequently to these Seas. The Weapons and*

Arts

Arts which they ſaw, beyond thoſe of other Sauages are arguments hereof. Hee which aſſaulted *Pricket* in the Boate, had a weapon broad and ſharpe indented of bright Steele (ſuch they vſe in *Iaua*) riueted into a handle of Morſe tooth.

Chap. XVIII.

The Diſcoueries of M. M. Nicolo, *and* Antonio Zeni, *gathered out of their Letters, by* Francisco Marcolino : *whereto is added* Qvirino *his Ship-wracke.*

They are related by Maſter Hakluit, in his 3.vol pag 121.

Friſland.

 N the yeere 1380. Maſter *Nicolo Zeno* being wealthy, and of a haughtie ſpirit, deſiring to ſee the faſhions of the world, built and furniſhed a Ship at his owne charges, and paſſing the Straits of *Gibralter*, held on his courſe Northwards, with intent to ſee *England* and *Flanders*. But a violent tempeſt aſſailing him at Sea, hee was carried hee knew not whither, till at laſt his Ship was carried away vpon the Ile of *Friſland* ; where the men and moſt part of the goods were ſaued. In vaine ſeemes that deliuerie, that deliuers vp preſently to another Executioner. The Ilanders like *Neptunes*, hungry groomes, or his baſe and blacke Guard, ſet vpon the men whom the Seas had ſpared : but heere alſo they found a ſecond eſcape, by meanes of a Prince named *Zichmni*, Prince of that and many Ilands thereabouts : who being neere hand with his Armie, came at the out-crie, and chaſing away the people, tooke them into protection.

This *Zichmni* had the yeere before giuen the ouerthrow to the King of *Norway*, and was a great aduenturer in feates of Armes. He ſpake to them in *Latine*, and placed them in his Nauie, wherewith hee wonne diuers Ilands. *Nicolo* behaued himſelfe ſo well, both in ſauing the Fleet by his Sea-skill, and in conqueſt of the Ilands by his valour, that *Zichmni* made him Knight and Captaine of his Nauie.

Saint Thomas Monaſterie in Groenland. Hote Spring and the ſtrange effects thereof.

After diuers notable exploits, *Nicolo* armed three Barkes, with which hee arriued in *Engroneland* : where hee found a Monaſterie of Friers of the *Preachers* Order, and a Church dedicated to Saint *Thomas*, hard by a Hill, that caſteth out fire like *Veſuuius* and *Ætna*. There is a Fountaine of hot water, with which they heate the Church of the Monaſterie, and the Friers chambers. It commeth alſo into the Kitchin ſo boyling hote, that they vſe no other fire to dreſſe their meate; and putting their Bread into braſſe Pots without any water, it doth bake as it were in an hot Ouen. They haue alſo ſmall Gardens, which are couered ouer in the Winter time, and being watered with this water, are defended from the violence of the Froſt and cold, and bring forth Flowers in their due ſeaſons. The common people aſtoniſhed with theſe ſtrange effects, conceiue highly of thoſe Friers, and bring them preſents of Fleſh and other things. They with this Water, in the extremitie of the cold, heate their Chambers, which alſo (as the other buildings of the Monaſterie) are framed of thoſe burning ſtones, which the mouth of the Hill caſts foorth. They caſt water on ſome of them, whereby they are diſſolued, and become excellent white Lime, and ſo tough, that being contriued in building, it laſteth for euer. The reſt, after the fire is out, ſerue in ſtead of ſtones to make walls and vaults, and will not diſſolue or breake, except with ſome Iron toole.

Their Winter laſteth nine moneths : and yet there is a faire Hauen, where this water falleth into the Sea, not frozen : by meanes whereof there is great reſort of wild Fowle and Fiſh, which they take in infinite multitudes. The Fiſhers Boates are made like to a Weauers ſhuttle, of the skinnes of Fiſhes, faſhioned with the bones of the ſame Fiſhes, and being ſowed together with many doubles, they are ſo ſtrong, that in foule weather they will ſhut themſelues within the ſame, not fearing the force either of Sea or winde. Neither can the hard-hearted Rockes breake theſe yeelding Veſſels. They haue alſo as it were a Sleeue in the bottome thereof, by which with a ſubtill deuice, they conuey the water foorth, that ſoaketh into them. The moſt of theſe Friers ſpake the *Latine* tongue.

Eſtotiland.

A little after this, *Nicolo* returned and dyed in *Friſland*, whither his brother *Antonio* had before reſorted to him, and now ſucceeded both in his goods and honour ; whom *Zichmni* employed in the Expedition of *Eſtotiland* : which happened vpon this occaſion. Sixe and twentie yeeres before, foure Fiſher-Boates were apprehended at Sea by a mightie and tedious ſtorme; wherewith after many dayes, they were brought to *Eſtotiland*, aboue a thouſand miles Weſt from *Friſland* : vpon which, one of the Boates was caſt away, and ſixe men that were in it, were taken and brought to a populous Citie ; where, one that ſpake *Latine*, and had been caſt by chance vpon that Iland, in the name of the King asked them what Country-men they were; and vnderſtanding their caſe, hee acquainted the King therewith. They dwelt there fiue yeeres, and found it to bee an Iland very rich, being little leſſe then *Iſeland*, but farre more fruitfull. One of them ſaid hee ſaw *Latine* bookes in the Kings Librarie, which they at this preſent doe not vnderſtand.

stand. They haue a peculiar Language, and Letters or Characters to themselues. They haue mines of Gold and other Mettals, and haue Trade with *Engroneland.* They sow Corne, and make Beere and Ale. They build Barkes (but know not the vse of the Compasse) and haue many Cities and Castles. The King sent these Fisher-men with twelue Barkes Southwards, to a Countrey which they call *Drogio :* in which Voyage escaping dreadfull tempests at Sea, they encountred with *Canibals* at Land, which deuoured many of them. These Fishers shewing them the manner of taking Fish with Nets, escaped, and for the presents which they made of their Fish to the chiefe men of the Country, were beloued and honoured. One of these (more expert it seemeth then the rest) was holden in such account, that a great Lord made warre with their Lord to obtaine him : and so preuayled, that he and his companie were sent vnto him. And in this order was hee sent to fiue and twentie Lords, which had warred one with another to get him, in thirteene yeeres space : whereby hee came to know almost all those parts ; which, he said, was a great Countrey, and (as it were) a new World. The people are all rude, and voide of goodnesse : they goe naked, neither haue they wit to couer their bodies with the Beasts skinnes which they take in Hunting, from the vehement cold. They are fierce, and eate their enemies, hauing diuers Lawes and Gouernours. Their liuing is by hunting.

Further to the South-west, they are more ciuill, and haue a more temperate ayre : They haue Cities and Temples dedicated to Idols, where they sacrifice Men, and after eate them; and haue also some vse of Gold and Siluer.

Hee fledde away secretly, and conueying himselfe from one Lord to another, came at length to *Drogio,* where hee dwelt three yeeres. After this time finding there certaine Boates of *Estotiland,* hee went thither with them : and growing there very rich, furnished a Barke of his owne, and returned into *Friesland :* where hee made report vnto his Lord of that wealthy Countrey. *Zichmui* prepared to send thither : but three dayes before they set foorth, this Fisherman dyed. Yet taking some of the Marriners which came with him in his stead, they prosecuted the Voyage, and encountred after many dayes an Iland ; where ten men of diuers Languages, were brought vnto them, of which they could vnderstand none, but one of *Iseland.* Hee told them, that the Iland was called *Icaria,* and the Knights thereof called *Icars,* descended of the ancient pedigree of *Dedalus,* King of *Scots,* who conquering that Iland, left his Sonne there for King, and left them those Lawes, which to that present they retayned. And, that they might keepe their Lawes inuiolate, they would receiue no Stranger. Onely they were contented to receiue one of our men, in regard of the Language, as they had done those ten Interpreters.

Zichmui sayling hence, in foure dayes descried Land, where they found abundance of Fowle, and Birds egges, for their refreshing. The Hauen they called Cap *Trin.* There was a Hill, which burning, cast out smoake : where was a Spring, from which issued a certayne water like Pitch, which ranne into the Sea. The people of small stature, wilde, and fearefull, hid themselues in Caues. *Zichmui* built there a Citie, and determining to inhabite, sent *Antonio* backe againe, with the most of his people to *Friesland.*

This Historie I haue thus inserted at large, which perhaps, not without cause in some things, may seeme fabulous ; not in the *Zeni,* which thus writ, but in the relations which they receiued from others. Howsoeuer, the best Geographers are beholden to these Brethren, for that little knowledge they haue of these parts ; of which none before had written : nor since haue there beene any great in-land Discoueries.

Abrah.Ortel. chart.6. Hakwol3. Botero. Magnus. Hondius, &c.

The Ship-wracke of Master PIERO QVIRINO, described by CHRISTOFORO FIORAVANTI, and NICOLO DI MICHIEL*, who were present there : heere contracted.

IT semeth to bee a conuenient dutie to make a memoriall, and not suffer to bee buryed in obliuion, that most lamentable, and cruell Voyage full of innumerable and extreame miseries, which befell a *Venetian* Ship, wherein wee carryed about seuen hundred Buttes of Wine, Spices, Cottons, and other Merchandises of great value, furnished in *Candia* with threescore and eight men, to goe towards the * West. The Master whereof was Master *Piero Quirini,* a *Venetian* Gentleman, in the yeare 1431. Who after many troubles *, misfortunes, and wants betalne him, after his departure from *Candia* towards the West, on the sixth of Nouember, in the foresaid yeere of the Lord, by chance came into the mouth of the Channels of *Flanders,* and went farre beyond them, by a storme from the South, towards the North-west, about one hundred and fortie miles, running still vpon the Iland of *Vssenti,* where, by agreement, wee *Christoforo Fiorauanti,* and *Nicolo Michiel,* say, that at noone wee sounded the bottome of the ocean, and these parts the Ponent or West. * These are particularly related by *Quirino* the Patron or Owner. They lost their Rudder on a Rocke, not farre from *Cales* in *Spaine,* and were faine to make thither to repaire it : and other draft rs followed.

*There is also the relation hereof by Quirino himselfe, extant together with this in Famusio, Tom 2. Out of which I haue heere added diuers annotations. * The Italians call the Syring into the Mediterraneas the Leuant or East; and thence int the Spanish Ocean.*

Sea